Edo Painting:
Sotatsu and Korin

Volume 18

THE HEIBONSHA SURVEY OF JAPANESE ART

For a list of the entire series see end of book

CONSULTING EDITORS

Katsuichiro Kamei, *art critic*
Seiichiro Takahashi, *Chairman, Japan Art Academy*
Ichimatsu Tanaka, *Chairman, Cultural Properties Protection Commission*

Edo Painting: Sotatsu and Korin

by HIROSHI MIZUO

translated by John M. Shields

New York • WEATHERHILL/HEIBONSHA • Tokyo

This book was originally published in Japanese by Heibonsha under the title *Sotatsu to Korin* in the Nihon no Bijutsu Series.

First English Edition, 1972
Second Printing, 1978

Jointly published by John Weatherhill, Inc., of New York and Tokyo, with editorial offices at 7–6–13 Roppongi, Minato-ku, Tokyo 106, and Heibonsha, Tokyo. Copyright © 1965, 1972, by Heibonsha; all rights reserved. Printed in Japan.

L C C Card No. 72-79122   I S B N 0–8348–1011–5

Contents

Edo Painting:
Sotatsu and Korin

CHAPTER ONE

Four Masters of Decorative Art

ALTHOUGH THIS BOOK is titled *Edo Painting: Sotatsu and Korin*, it actually treats of four great artists. The other two are Hon'ami Koetsu and Ogata Kenzan. Koetsu, a giant of Japanese art, lived at the same time as Sotatsu. Kenzan was the younger brother of Korin. Together the Ogata brothers' beautiful work represents the flowering of Genroku-era (1688–1704) art.

Koetsu, Sotatsu, Korin, and Kenzan: four masters of decorative art—four reasons one feels fortunate to have been born in Japan. This is not only because of the tremendous artistic value of their many works but also because these embody the very essence of what is Japanese in Japanese art.

Art historians often call them and their followers the "school of decorative painting." Decorative painting may be defined as any painting in which decoration, in the broadest sense of the term, is involved. It embraces what are called *hekiga* (mural painting), *fusuma-e* (sliding-door painting), and *byobu-e* (screen painting) in buildings; the underpainting, called *shita-e*, done on special paper that is later inscribed with thirty-one-syllable *waka* poems or Buddhist sutras; and design painting on everyday articles, such as round or folding fans.

This is distinguished from what I would arbitrarily call the "pure painting" of the fine arts today, in which the artist tries to express his individuality directly and forcefully. "Decorative" in this sense thus describes most Japanese painting. Even religious painting, in addition to its devotional content, is decorative. Much of the ink painting of the Muromachi (1336–1568) and Edo (1603–1868) periods, though in many senses "pure painting," was also put to decorative use. Japanese painting in general thus has little of the "pure" or personalist quality found in the modern West, where painting is a matter of "art for art's sake" and individual expression is sought. Instead, it is fair to say that in Japan, by and large, painting has been wed to a given use. Hence, the painting of a Sotatsu or a Korin—representative of the decorative school in a land where all art is strongly decorative—embodies that which is basic to Japanese painting.

Discussion of the distinction between decorative and "pure" painting becomes unimportant once we move into the realm of the marvelous work of these four men. What is important is the way in which the work of each is a window on his world, how it is so original yet so universal as to be able to speak to everyone. All great art is at once original and universal. Discovering what makes for this originality and universality should be the incentive for and the pleasure in studying an artist's work. Koetsu, Sotatsu, Korin, and Kenzan, all four replete with both originality and universality, reach out to gladden and charm us with the compelling inner beauty of their art. By studying their work we can grasp the nature of decorative art, catch hold of that which truly shapes Japanese art, and discover beauty in concrete form.

Unfortunately, our sources of information are

very limited. We are forced to make do with a collage of their careers pasted together from scraps of information. Koetsu and Sotatsu lived about 350 years ago, from the end of the sixteenth century into the first half of the seventeenth century. Korin and Kenzan lived about fifty years later, in the late seventeenth century, when the Genroku era was well under way. Like us, they had their joys and sorrows and, moreover, seem to have had rather stormy careers. But we are left with few records. Life is fleeting; not to have been recorded is almost not to have lived at all. But in place of words we are left with an immense legacy of eloquent art. This makes their existence credible and, more than writing could ever do, clearly and truly communicates their inmost selves. Thus they live on, speaking to us through their work across space and time.

Scholars are constantly trying to turn up more and more information on these four figures. They sift and sort bits of accumulated data, building a hypothetical case like detectives, comparing this or that with these men's art, always endeavoring to give a better picture of them. The adequacy of the final picture, however, depends largely on our own judgment and sensitivity in viewing their art. I will try to trace their footsteps in an effort to sketch their profiles. I hope to go beyond explanation and artistic appreciation to the problem of seeing how each encountered his own time.

The sixteenth and seventeenth centuries were a time of great upheaval in Japan, followed by a period of relative peace. Whether in times of turmoil or of stability, the artist must confront reality and take an original stance. How, then, does a

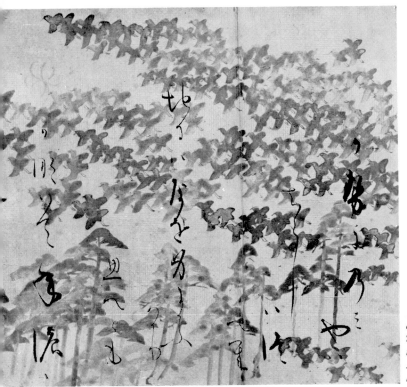

1. *Hon'ami Koetsu and Tawaraya Sotatsu: detail of* Flowers and Grasses of the Four Seasons. *Hand scroll with painting by Sotatsu and calligraphy by Koetsu. Gold-and-silver underpainting on paper; height, 34 cm.; length, 922.2 cm. Early seventeenth century.*

given mode of thought or life-style show up in the art of Koetsu, Sotatsu, Korin, and Kenzan? Were their works what they were out of some necessity? These are questions I would like to consider from the start.

THE LIVES of Hon'ami Koetsu and Tawaraya Sotatsu were inextricably interwoven. The Sugawara–Matsuda–Hon'ami family genealogy lists a cousin of Koetsu as the wife of Sotatsu. From this arose the view that they were blood relatives. The record is now lost and we have no way to verify this claim, but in any case, their relationship was deeper than that of blood.

I once ventured that Sotatsu might be another name for Koetsu. In other words, could they not have been one and the same person? Of course they were actually two different people, each of whom was a major figure in the history of Japanese art. The point of this fantasizing was to emphasize how close they were to each other. In the "Sotatsu's painting–Koetsu's script" masterpieces attributed to them—works with gold-and-silver underpainting on *waka* scrolls or *shikishi*, square sheets for poems or pictures—was it really Sotatsu who did the underpainting? Or was it Koetsu? Or was it perhaps both of them? Again, did Koetsu just have the idea and Sotatsu do the rest? All these points, subject to various interpretations, gave rise to my "same person" theory. What I was driving at was that these two men present an unprecedented situation in world art history—two men of incomparable talent working together in matchless artistic endeavor, either of whom could be thought capable of the

2. *Tawaraya Sotatsu: fan paintings mounted on a pair of eightfold screens. Colors on paper; dimensions of each screen: height, 111.5 cm.; width, 376 cm. Early seventeenth century. Imperial Household Collection. (See also Figure 138.)*

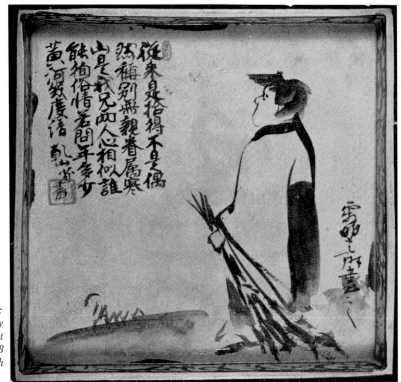

3. *Ogata Korin and Ogata Kenzan: square dish by Kenzan with calligraphy and painting of Shih-te by Korin. Rust painting; length, 21.8 cm.; width, 21.8 cm.; height, 2.8 cm. Early eighteenth century. Fujita Art Museum, Osaka.*

other's task in executing a joint masterpiece. In addition, we are saddled with the enigma of Sotatsu —an artist of great stature, yet of whose life next to nothing is known. How explain the riddle of the two save by the "same person" theory? This was the argument.

But all this aside, even though they were not actually one and the same person, there is little doubt they worked together, shared the same esthetic sense, and realized a single artistic ideal. Their combined creativity, in gold-and-silver painting and other media, achieved both a classical revival and a new decorative art. Let us look for indications of these achievements in their works.

CHAPTER TWO

The Art of Koetsu

CALLIGRAPHY Hon'ami Koetsu was born in 1558 and died in 1637. He was amazingly productive over a span of almost eighty years, excelling most in calligraphy. The style of writing that bears his name can be seen in numerous *shikishi*, *waka* scrolls (Figs. 1, 8, 17, 40, 68, 124, 128), sutra copies (Fig. 136), and letters (Fig. 4). It revolutionized calligraphy at a time when the *oie-ryu* (literally, "prince's style") script was standard. Koetsu based his writing on that of the Shoren-in school, with an added flourish from the master calligraphers of the Heian period (794–1185), Kukai (774–835) and Tofu (894–966). He also incorporated elements from the famed Chinese calligrapher who was often a model for Japanese writing, Wang Hsi-chih (321–79). Graceful, free, and refined, Koetsu's style was deeply Japanese in feeling. People acclaimed it along with the calligraphy of Konoe Sammyaku-in and Shokado Shojo as the three great scripts of the day. Koetsu himself is said to have implied that his own was the best.

His magnificent calligraphy is seen in his beautiful copies of *waka* from the *Kokinshu* and *Shin Kokin-shu* poetry anthologies, written over gold-and-silver underpainting in a script rivaling that of the Heian-period *Genji Monogatari* (Tale of Genji) and *Sanjurokunin-shu* poetry anthology. In fact, I would hold that Koetsu's style is far superior. To the classical verses and decorated paper he brought the perfect blend of Momoyama-period (1568–1603) sumptuousness, achieving an exquisite harmony of writing and painting. It was the quest for the old arts of Japan, the classical beauty of Heian, that informed Koetsu's writing style. The renaissance of this classical tradition, as interpreted by his unique vision, was the inspiration of his calligraphy.

THE SAGA BOOKS The printing of books known as Saga-*bon*, or Saga books, named for a district in northwestern Kyoto, helped to diffuse Koetsu's calligraphic style and also fulfilled another very important function. This was the publishing of such classics as the tenth-century *Ise Monogatari* (Tales of Ise) and the twelfth-century *Hojoki*. Other classics and the Kanze-school Noh songbooks (Fig. 5) were also printed. The books were designed by Koetsu and his disciple the merchant-calligrapher Suminokura Soan, and then were stylishly produced on excellent-quality paper, to the joy of the Kyoto elite. Koetsu obviously was attempting to familiarize the public with his beloved classics. The design was regal, calling the reader back to the beauty of old Japan.

Koetsu lived following the Muromachi period, in which Chinese culture had enjoyed a great boom. A native Japanese culture had taken definite shape in Kyoto in the latter half of the Heian period. But it was to wane in the Kamakura (1185–1336) and Muromachi periods under the strong Chinese influences of ink painting and Zen. Confronted with a debilitated Yamato-e, traditional Japanese-theme painting, and the vanishing elegance of the old

4. Hon'ami Koetsu: letter to Sotoku. Height, 28 cm.; width, 44.2 cm. C. 1620.

imperial culture, Koetsu found himself more and more harking back to Heian culture as a long-lost home. But this was no mere nostalgia. He looked back to Heian as the time when a truly Japanese culture had welled up from purely Japanese springs. Its beauty he saw clearly as a Japanese beauty, and he was convinced it was his destiny to follow the course of Japan's indigenous culture. As its heir, he would further it. This, I think, was the most important motivation in his life.

Koetsu's *waka* scrolls with gold-and-silver underpainting comprised especially luxurious Saga editions. The plant and animal motifs, representative of the decorative school, had been handed down from Heian times in traditional Yamato-e form. As with his transformation of *oie-ryu* calligraphy. Koetsu would reshape these ingredients into a style distinctively his own.

He began with fresh designs and techniques. Patterns were enlarged and enriched. With his gold-and-silver *betanuri* (complete painting of a surface)

technique, Koetsu created brilliant, patterned paintings in the Momoyama style. Revolutionary creations of decorative art, they were probably conceived and executed together with Sotatsu, who was both technically and esthetically equipped to execute the paintings without losing anything of Koetsu's vision. Among the gold-and-silver underpaintings, most of which were on *shikishi* paper or *waka* scrolls, we can discern Koetsu's brushwork in some. But by and large, I think, it was through Sotatsu that Koetsu realized his dreams; and it was through knowing Koetsu that Sotatsu could best utilize his technical resources.

CERAMICS AND LACQUERWARE
Koetsu was also extremely accomplished in ceramics and lacquerware. These require craftsman's skills and, unlike painting, deal in three-dimensional forms. Here the individuality of Koetsu comes sharply to the fore. His tea bowls are reputed to be the culmination of Raku ware, a

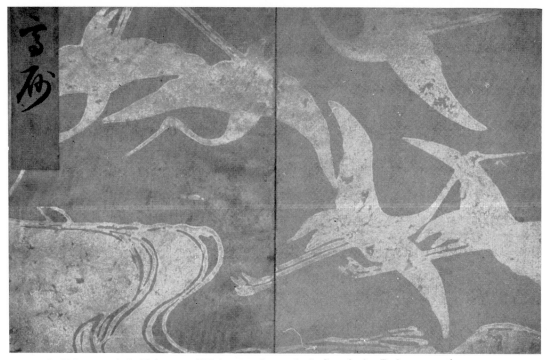

5. Noh songbook for Takasago. *Third group of songs in the Saga books. Early seventeenth century.*

rustic style of pottery originated by the Raku family; and his inkstone cases are acclaimed as a revolution in lacquerware. The treatment of design and shape is bold, rugged, and intense, distilling both the personality of Koetsu and his esthetic sense. Here one finds, just as in his gold-and-silver painting, the ideal of the traditional form of Japanese beatuy.

His celebrated tea bowls "Mount Fuji" (Fig. 24), "Autumn Shower" (Fig. 126), "Rain Clouds" (Fig. 127), and "Bishamondo" (Figs. 21, 22) display an artistry and feeling quite distinct from those of China or Korea; one is apt to be dazzled by their sheer strength of form. In shape, handling of glaze, and the variety and richness of the whole, no

tea bowls embody as clearly as those of Koetsu that which is distinctively Japanese. A regal elegance flows uninterrupted beneath the Momoyama decoration.

Koetsu's gold lacquerwork indicates again his longing for the classical past. His "Boat-bridge" inkstone case (Fig. 26) has an old poem on it; the "Boat in the Reeds" case design (Fig. 25) is borrowed from Yamato-e, but Koetsu transformed it with his novel techniques and shapes. This fresh kind of gold lacquerware must have seemed quite avant-garde for the times. The updated design made what was old look so new that it went entirely unrecognized as being old. This is worlds apart from the New Wave of today, which tries so hard

6. Tawaraya Sotatsu: detail of Matsushima. *Pair of sixfold screens. Colors on gold foil over paper; dimensions of each screen:* ▷
height, 166 cm.; width, 370 cm. Early seventeenth century. Freer Gallery of Art, Washington, D.C. (See also Figure 135.)

7. *Tawaraya Sotatsu:* Bugaku. *Pair of twofold screens. Colors on gold foil over paper; dimensions of each screen: height, 155 cm.; width, 169 cm. Early seventeenth century. Sambo-in, Daigo-ji, Kyoto. (See also Figure 67.)*

8. *Hon'ami Koetsu and Tawaraya Sotatsu: detail of* Flowers and Grasses of the Four Seasons. *Hand scroll with painting by Sotatsu and calligraphy by Koetsu. Gold-and-silver underpainting on paper; height, 33.7 cm.; length, 924.1 cm. Early seventeenth century. Hatakeyama Kinenkan, Tokyo.*

9. *Tawaraya Sotatsu:* Flowers and Grasses. *Four-panel sliding doors. Colors on gold foil over paper; dimensions of each panel: height, 170 cm.; width, 94 cm. C. mid-seventeenth century.*

10. *Tawaraya Sotatsu: "Miotsukushi" scene (above) and "Sekiya" scene from Genji*
Monogatari. *Pair of sixfold screens. Colors on gold foil over paper; dimensions of each*
screen: height, 152.3 cm.; width, 355.6 cm. C. mid-seventeenth century. Seikado, Tokyo.

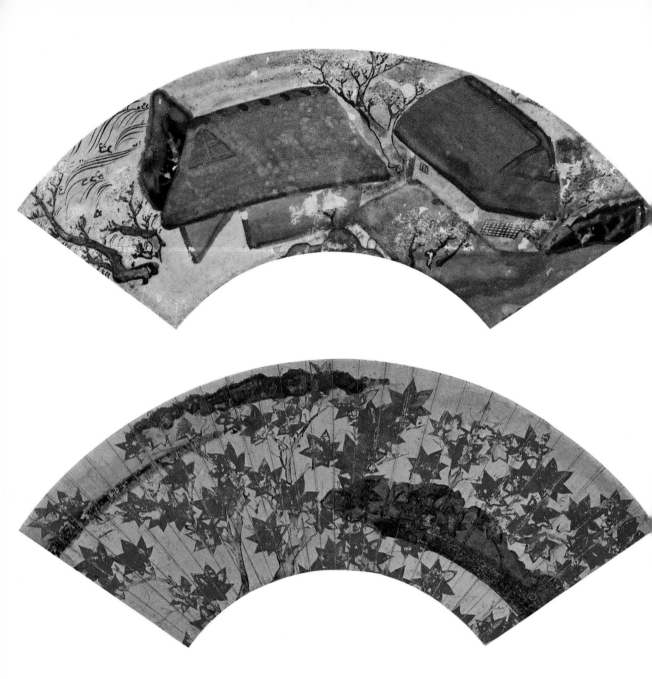

11 (above). Tawaraya Sotatsu: Farmhouses in Spring. *Fan painting mounted on a panel of a pair of twofold screens. Colors on paper; height, 18 cm.; width, 57 cm. Early seventeenth century. Sambo-in, Daigo-ji, Kyoto. (See also Figure 133.)*

12 (below). Tawaraya Sotatsu: Maples. *Fan painting mounted on a panel of a pair of sixfold screens. Colors on gold foil over paper; height, 17.8 cm.; width, 63.3 cm. Early seventeenth century. Myoho-in, Kyoto.*

13. Tawaraya Sotatsu: "Battle of Rokugahara" scene from Heiji Monogatari. *Fan paintings mounted on a panel of a pair of* ▷ *sixfold screens. Colors on paper; height, 19 cm.; width, 59 cm. Early seventeenth century. Imperial Household Collection, Tokyo.*

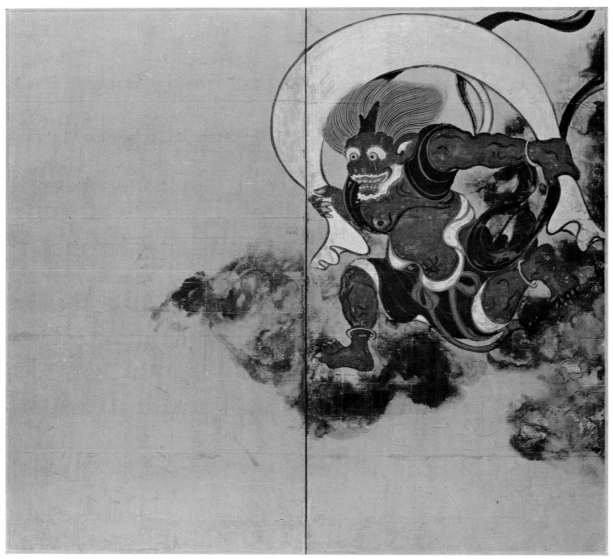

14. Tawaraya Sotatsu: God of Wind and God of Thunder. *Pair of twofold screens. Colors on gold foil over paper; dimensions of each screen: height, 154.5 cm.; width, 169.8 cm. Mid-seventeenth century. Kennin-ji, Kyoto.*

15. *Tawaraya Sotatsu: detail of* Life of Priest Saigyo. *Hand scroll. Colors on paper; height, 33.4 cm. 1630. Formerly in the Mori Collection. (See also Figure 42.)*

16 *(below). Tawaraya Sotatsu: detail of* Life of Priest Saigyo. *Hand scroll. Colors on paper; height, 32.7 cm. 1630. Watanabe Collection.*

18. *Tawaraya Sotatsu: Lion. One of four cedar doors. Colors on wood; height, 181 cm.; width, 125 cm. C. 1621. Yogen-in, Kyoto.*

◁ *17. Hon'ami Koetsu and Tawaraya Sotatsu: detail of Deer. Hand scroll with painting by Koetsu and Sotatsu and calligraphy by Koetsu. Gold-and-silver underpainting on paper; height, 34.7 cm.; length, 428 cm. Early seventeenth century. Atami Art Museum, Shizuoka Prefecture.*

19. Tawaraya Sotatsu: Ise Monogatari *scene. Shikishi. Colors on paper; height, 24.6 cm.; width, 21 cm. Early seventeenth century.*

20. *Hon'ami Koetsu: writing box. Inlay on black and gold lacquer; length, 24.4 cm.; width, 23 cm.; height, 10.8 cm. Early seventeenth century. Atami Art Museum, Shizuoka Prefecture.*

21. *Hon'ami Koetsu: "Bishamondo" tea bowl. Red Raku ware; diameter, 11.7 cm. Early seventeenth century. (See also Figure 22).*

" *Genji Monogatari*

Kitano Tenjin Engi

old Bugaku screens

Bugaku

SOTATSU
OF CON

Sotatsu's comp
treatment of a
which he perfec
Tawaraya, then
faces. The me
elements: radia
at lower cente
series of arcs,
right to left. T
inherited in a
from Heian-
finally perfect

God of Wind an

God of Thunder   *Kitano Tenjin Engi*

God of Thunder

Musashino

Flowers and Grasses

Flowers and Grasses

osition is based on the
a folding-fan surface,
ted in his work at the
e applied to large sur-
thod comprises three
tion from the fan pivot
r, development in a
and progression from
ese elements had been
unbroken tradition
iod fans and were
by Sotatsu.

od of Thunder

Genji Monogatari

"Sekiya,

Farmhouses in Spring

Bamboo

Advent of Amida

sutra fan painting

The four examples with red lines superimposed show Sotatsu's application of fan composition to large surfaces. Comparison with older works from which Sotatsu drew his themes and with works not using the fan-composition approach show the superiority of Sotatsu's treatment. It is this method that gives the *Bugaku* composition both coherence and depth. Sotatsu's *Genji* screens show a more intricate application of the principles of fan composition. These also give the *Flowers and Grasses* doors a feeling of life and expansiveness and endow the *God of Wind and God of Thunder* screens with a freedom not seen in earlier renditions. While he remains faithful to the principles of fan composition, Sotatsu's feeling soars into a realm of limitless space.

22. Hon'ami Koetsu: "Bishamondo" tea bowl. Red Raku ware; diameter, 11.7 cm. Early seventeenth century. (See also Figure 21.)

23 (right). Hon'ami Koho: wood carving of Koetsu. C. mid-seventeenth century.

to be new by divorcing itself from tradition. The techniques used in the billowed cover of the "Boat-bridge" case, with its lead and mother-of-pearl inlay, had already been tried by lacquer artisans. Koetsu, like Sotatsu, used the skills of these craftsmen to the fullest in realizing his creations.

KOETSU COULD NEVER have undertaken the work he did without a good grasp of the crafts, a keen sense of beauty, and a thorough knowledge and appreciation of the classics. He was groomed for his task by the Hon'ami family business, which consisted in the cleaning, polishing, and connoisseurship of swords. The *Hon'ami Family Annals* (Hon'ami Gyojoki) record that Koetsu was raised and encouraged in the trade from early childhood and that he became a master at it. This enhanced his appreciation of beauty and fostered his technique, as well. In Japan, to sound the secrets of sword-craft is to lay claim to the best of craftsmanship.

And we can easily imagine Koetsu to have had an eye sharp as a shining sword edge, able to pierce and lay bare beauty's secrets. His eye was to fix on what he believed to be the highest beauty—the classical beauty of Heian Japan. Its renaissance would be his vocation.

Koetsu's towering, many-faceted work and his zealous commitment to classicism far exceeded the normal range of interests of the stratum of wealthy upper-class merchants to which he belonged. His exceptional talent and sensitivity went far beyond those of the dilettante. Something more compelling inspired his heights of creativity. There is also the evidence of Takagamine Koetsu Village, the community he formed on land given to him by the shogun Tokugawa Ieyasu in 1615. Koetsu moved to this plot in northeastern Kyoto along with his family and a host of craftsmen and friends from among the upper-class *machishu*, wealthy merchants who often supported cultural activities.

24. Hon'ami Koetsu: "Mount Fuji" tea bowl. White Raku ware. Diameter, 11.6 cm. Early seventeenth century.

25. Hon'ami Koetsu: inkstone case with design of a boat in the reeds. Gold lacquer; length, 23.7 cm.; width, 22.3 cm.; height, 4.2 cm. Early seventeenth century. Tokyo National Museum.

26. *Hon'ami Koetsu: "Boat-bridge" inkstone case. Lead and mother-of-pearl on gold lacquer; length, 24.2 cm.; width, 22.7 cm.; height, 11.8 cm. Early seventeenth century. Tokyo National Museum.*

Here he presided over artistic production. Many of his fine gold-and-silver paintings, gold lacquerwork, and tea bowls are thought to have been made here. An old map of Takagamine (Fig. 55) gives us the names of Kamiya Soji (a paper maker), Fudeya Myoki (a brush maker), and well-known lacquer artisans. It is not hard to guess why Koetsu pursued his creative activities through Takagamine Koetsu Village. It embodied his personal creed as man and artist. Let us keep this in mind as we now take a general look at the artistic achievements of his great contemporary, Sotatsu.

CHAPTER THREE

The Art of Sotatsu

MAN OF MYSTERY   It is only natural to expect that because of his close connection with Koetsu, the thought and work of Sotatsu would have much in common with Koetsu's. For sources on Koetsu, we have the *Hon'ami Family Annals* and references in the *Nigiwahiso* by Haiya Shoeki, a pupil of Koetsu, to inform us of his philosophy and activities. Sotatsu, on the other hand, is almost wholly wrapped in mystery. We know the date of neither his birth nor his death, nor even his family background. The only works dated and thus indisputably his are the *Hamamatsu* fan painting of 1607 (Fig. 32) and a *Life of Priest Saigyo* scroll of 1630 (Figs. 15, 42). The only other clues are attributions: a restoration of the frontispiece of the *Heike Nokyo* scrolls in the Itsukushima Shrine near Hiroshima, dated 1602 (Fig. 136), and the cedar doors in the Yogen-in temple in Kyoto, dated 1621 (Figs. 18, 38).

Painstaking research offers a few more bits of information: that the renowned Tawaraya of Kyoto, a fan-making establishment, was his; that he first met Koetsu around 1605; that he received commissions for court work from Emperor Gomizuno-o (r. 1611–29) and Karasumaru Mitsuhiro; that he apparently was versed in tea ceremony; and that he reached the rank of *hokkyo* (a Buddhist term designating a high rank for eminent painters).

All this tells us that Sotatsu was a person of no mean social standing; but his character, philosophy, and esthetics can only be conjectured from his works. Possibly the only other truly great painter of post-medieval times equally as mysterious is the famed eighteenth-century *ukiyo-e* print artist Sharaku.

FAN PAINTING   *Chikusai*, a book written c. 1623 by Isoda Doji, is a description of famous places of interest. In it is the following passage: "The Kyoto fan-maker Tawaraya has done lavish illustrations of fans from the 'Yugao' tale of Hikaru Genji." When we consider this and the many fans that have come down to us from Sotatsu, the case is all but conclusive that he was the master of the Tawaraya. The best of his work in this genre is seen in the screen-mounted fans in the Sambo-in at Daigo-ji temple, Kyoto (Figs. 11, 29, 133), and in the Imperial Household Collection (Figs. 2, 13, 134, 138).

The way that Sotatsu handled a painting surface shows the practiced hand of a master. The reason he is sometimes called "modern" is largely due to his approach to composition. And it was the fan medium that was the matrix of his sense of composition and technique. In his fan-compositional approach we see three major elements. First, the composition radiates from the fan pivot, which serves as the center; second, everything revolves around this central pivot; and third, there is a progressive movement from right to left, like a scroll unrolling horizontally. No other artist has so skillfully combined these three elements.

27. *Tawaraya Sotatsu: "Azuma Kudari" scene from* Ise Monogatari. Shikishi. *Colors on paper; height, 24.4 cm.; width, 20.7 cm. Early seventeenth century.*

28. *Tawaraya Sotatsu: "Ivy Walk" scene from* Ise Monogatari. Shikishi. *Colors on paper; height, 24.7 cm.; width, 21 cm. Early seventeenth century.*

A variety of such fans, with all kinds of themes, was produced and sold throughout Kyoto, giving the Tawaraya quite a reputation. This expertise in handling fan surfaces was to be the basis for the marvelous composition of Sotatsu's later, large-surface paintings. The Sotatsu of *hokkyo* stature would be inconceivable without the Sotatsu of the Tawaraya, the master of fancraft.

The Tawaraya was a decorative-painting atelier. This kind of business, in which a number of craftsmen produced paintings for sale, was called an *e-ya* —literally, "painting shop." Tawaraya work was not limited to fan painting. The establishment also turned out underpaintings on *shikishi* and *waka* scroll paper, screen paintings, and paintings on paper to be mounted on screens. It is probable that the Tawaraya was also equipped to do woodblock printing. To each and every task Sotatsu had to

bring a skilled hand. Folding scroll book illustrations on *shikishi* of themes from the *Ise Monogatari;* block-printed underpaintings of flowers and grasses; ink paintings mounted on screens; gold-and-silver-painted *waka* scroll paper—all these were among the rich products of the prolific Sotatsu and his Tawaraya.

SCREENS Sotatsu's large surfaces, painted in rich colors on a gold ground, come to mind as his most representative works. His three greatest works, the *Genji Monogatari* screens (Fig. 10), the *Bugaku* (Court Dance) screens (Figs. 7, 67), and the *God of Wind and God of Thunder* screens (Fig. 14), are masterpieces for their economy of composition, richness of portrayal, and harmony of deep and brilliant hues. These three works went beyond a revival of Yamato-e to originate an utterly new

29. *Tawaraya Sotatsu: fan painting of dogs mounted on a panel of a pair of twofold screens. Colors on paper. Sambo-in, Daigo-ji, Kyoto. (See also Figure 133.)*

30. *Sotatsu school: fan painting of a* Heiji Monogatari *scene mounted on a panel of a pair of sixfold screens. Colors on gold foil over paper; height, 19 cm.; width, 56 cm. Early seventeenth century.*

31. *Tawaraya Sotatsu: fan painting of a Shinto shrine building mounted on a panel of a pair of sixfold screens. Colors on gold foil over paper; height, 18.5 cm.; width, 55.5 cm. Early seventeenth century.*

32. *Tawaraya Sotatsu:* Hamamatsu. *Fan painting mounted on a hanging scroll. Colors on gold foil over paper; height, 17.3 cm.; width, 51.5 cm. 1607.*

33. *Sotatsu school:* hamamatsu *scene on a fan painted directly on a panel of a pair of sixfold screens. Colors on gold foil over paper; height, 17.2 cm.; width, 53.2 cm. Early seventeenth century. Okura Cultural Foundation, Tokyo.*

34. *Sotatsu school: painting of waves on a fan painted directly on a panel of a pair of sixfold screens. Colors on gold foil over paper; height, 17.5 cm.; width, 55.7 cm. Early seventeenth century. Okura Cultural Foundation, Tokyo.*

35. *Sotatsu school: painting of peonies on a fan painted directly on a panel of a pair of sixfold screens. Colors on gold foil over paper; height, 17.8 cm.; width, 57 cm. Early seventeenth century. Okura Cultural Foundation, Tokyo.*

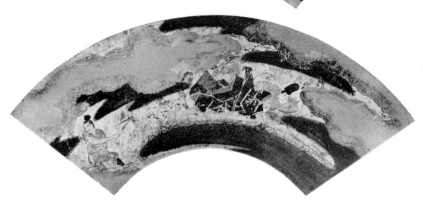

36. *Tawaraya Sotatsu:* Ise Monogatari *scene. Fan painting mounted on a panel of a pair of sixfold screens. Colors on gold foil over paper; height, 18.5 cm.; width, 56 cm. Early seventeenth century.*

decorative painting form that is valued as having created a Japanese art of tremendous fertility.

Moreover, if we count the *Matsushima* screens (Figs. 6, 135), the *Ivy Walk* screens (Fig. 41), the *Musashino* screens (Fig. 37), the sliding-door panels painted with flowers and grasses and bearing the Tawaraya's official Inen seal (Fig. 9), and the cedar doors of the Yogen-in temple (Figs. 18, 38), we see the almost infinite potential of Sotatsu's art, so rich and compelling are the sweep and sense of beauty it displays.

The fan painter–artisan, through a trade that nurtured his genius, rose to become the artist *hokkyo*. Yet more than talent, of course, went into this great artistic achievement. Few men of his talent were as steeped as Sotatsu in the classics, or as stimulated by a profession that continually demanded fresh ideas. Sotatsu diligently studied the Japanese art classics, such as the *Kitano Tenjin Engi*

scroll, paintings of the Hogen and Heiji wars, fifteenth-century Bugaku paintings, and the *Genji* and *Ise* scrolls. He studiously analyzed and endeavored to reproduce them, re-creating them in the process. This nurtured him as an artist, inculcating in him a love of classical Yamato-e and the world from which it sprang. This study would come to perfection, through his collaboration with Koetsu, in all but flawless painting.

His monumental achievement comprised not only color painting but also such ink-painting masterpieces as *Birds in a Lotus Pond* (Fig. 47) and *Oxen* (Fig. 45), which radically transformed ink painting. This medium had been showing gradual signs of becoming more Japanese in feeling since Kamakura times, and now under Sotatsu it took on an unmistakably Japanese quality.

What is the overall impression that one receives from this quick glance at Sotatsu's art? The pre-

37. *Tawaraya Sotatsu: detail of* Musashino. *Pair of sixfold screens. Colors on gold dust over paper; dimensions of each screen: height, 154.3 cm.; width, 364.4 cm. Late sixteenth century.*

eminence of his talent stands out, of course, but that is only stating the obvious. His amazing sense of composition deserves special remark: it easily fielded the challenge of all kinds of surfaces—fans, *shikishi*, hand scrolls, hanging scrolls, sliding-door panels, and screens. Then there is his delicate, balanced distribution of rich, deep colors. These are all salient characteristics of Sotatsu's art. He is a model of how an artist can be original, yet stand on tradition all the while. Yet however true this may be, and as deeply affected by him as we are even at some 350 years' remove, let us retrace our footsteps, this time to consider not so much what Sotatsu did as what he failed to do.

THE REVIVAL OF CLASSICAL BEAUTY

Both Sotatsu and Koetsu strove to revive and transform classical beauty. But Sotatsu's was the more pronounced attachment to the past. His devotion bordered on a sort of classical encapsulation, the subject matter being themes from *monogatari*, or tale, literature (*Ise, Genji, Saigyo*); landscapes and famous places from the tales; and flowers-and-grasses paintings, which were central to the Yamato-e tradition. He seems never to have concerned himself with depicting the life and manners of his own times—the field of *fuzokuga*, or genre painting.

Genre painting was very popular, especially during the Momoyama period. But Sotatsu was quite indifferent to it. This may have been due to the craftsman's nature of his work, but still, he was an artist whose business it was to sell paintings to the general public, and his never having done a single genre painting is worthy of remark.

It can be argued that Sotatsu and Koetsu were not alone in their abstention from genre art. Sesshu (1420–1506), the exemplar of *suibokuga* art; Yusho

38. *Tawaraya Sotatsu: painting of a white elephant on one of a pair of cedar doors. Colors on wood; dimensions of each door: height, 181 cm.; width, 125 cm. C. 1621. Yogen-in, Kyoto.*

39. *Tawaraya Sotatsu:* Thousand Cranes. *Pair of* shikishi. *Gold-and-silver underpainting on paper; dimensions of each* shikishi: *height, 18.1 cm.; width, 17 cm. Early seventeenth century. Goto Art Museum, Tokyo.*

(1533–1615), the founder of the Kaiho school; and Togan (1547–1618), a follower of Sesshu's ink-painting style, apparently did no such work, either. And nothing of the kind by the famous ink painter Tohaku (1539–1610) has been discovered.

With Koetsu and Sotatsu there were definite reasons for eschewing genre painting. First of all, Sotatsu stubbornly stuck to his classical world, making a conscious rejection of genre painting at a time when even the master painter Kano Eitoku (1543–90) was doing *Rakuchu, Rakugai*—screen paintings of contemporary scenes in and around Kyoto (Fig. 56). People were interested in contemporary painting; genre art was even represented in the decorative art inside Nagoya Castle. Sotatsu kept himself firmly aloof from all this; and the exquisite irony is that his first love, the world of the classic *monogatari* and Yamato-e, was in fact no more nor less than the genre world of the Heian period.

Yamato-e was simply the depiction of the manners and customs of a former time. Is it not strange then that someone so deeply imbued with tradition as Sotatsu should not have seen his way clear to do genre painting of his own times?

Second, and more important, Koetsu and Sotatsu came from the new upper-class merchant elite of Kyoto, the *machishu*. We will go into more detail about this emerging class in the following chapter. Suffice it to say here that the *machishu* were people who lived very much in the present. Self-assured, successful businessmen, they took pride in their life-style and carved out a culture of their own. Just as the Muromachi establishment had patronized and cultivated the Kano school of painters, this new elite aligned itself with the town painters, encouraging and patronizing them. These artists painted floral and *monogatari* themes, landscapes, and genre motifs. Even before the Kano school had popu-

40. *Hon'ami Koetsu and Tawaraya Sotatsu: detail of* Lotus *hand scroll with painting by Sotatsu and calligraphy by Koetsu. Gold-and-silver underpainting on paper; height, 33.3 cm. Early seventeenth century.*

larized genre painting, the town painters had been doing this kind of work.

The genre vogue cut across the lifetime of Sotatsu. In and around the Kan'ei era (1624–44), many so-called "Kan'ei *fuzokuga*" were produced, most of which were town-painter works commissioned by the *machishu*. Why Sotatsu and his Tawaraya artisans, the very cream of the town painters, could not bring themselves to tap the rich genre market is worth examining.

Was it that Koetsu and Sotatsu were so completely absorbed in their classic revival that they had no time for genre? It would hardly seem so. Nor is it persuasive to say that their customers, coming as they did from the nobility and the court, disdained

the vulgar taste for genre painting among the *nouveaux riches*. There must be a more telling reason both for the rush into a classical renaissance and the aversion to genre. Think about it: the classicism of Koetsu and his Takagamine Village, and the classicism of Sotatsu and his indifference to genre. Here we have a key that is not apparent in their works, one that can be traced back to a certain shared attitude toward the times in which they lived.

It was the early Edo period, the dawn of modern history in Japan. We have recognized Koetsu and Sotatsu for the magnificent quality of their works. Let us now probe the significance that the times held for them and for the Kyoto *machishu* to which they belonged.

CHAPTER FOUR

Koetsu, Sotatsu, and *Machishu* Culture

EMERGENCE OF THE
MACHISHU

The rise of the *machishu* of Kyoto came as an immediate aftermath of the ten-year Onin Civil War in the late fifteenth century. How did this new merchant class come to power? Thanks to the research of the eminent historian Tatsusaburo Hayashiya, we can obtain the following rough picture.

The new moneyed class was molded by a powerful group of sakè brewers and money dealers. They took articles in pawn and advanced money at usurious rates. They also collected taxes and thus received government protection. Having joined forces with the Muromachi government, they oppressed the farming class, obtaining immense landholdings. The farmers often revolted and, to stave off exploitation, formed self-governing organizations.

Confronted with agrarian uprisings, the merchants were put on the defensive. The Onin Civil War and enfeebled Muromachi policing left Kyoto in a state of confusion. Eventually the sakè brewers and pawnbrokers, along with various other business people, gravitated toward one another for mutual aid. This resulted in the formation of the guilds that knitted together most of Kyoto's merchant class. It was from the guilds that the *machishu* emerged. As a group, they took it upon themselves to maintain the

peace and preserve law and order, and so foster business. They were to Kyoto after the Onin Civil War what merchants were to Venice in late medieval times: they established what was in effect a free republic.

Life was exciting in Kyoto right after the civil war. The Muromachi government, the *bakufu*, was no more than a name; freedom and independence were anyone's for the taking. The great leaders of the period—Oda Nobunaga, Toyotomi Hideyoshi, Tokugawa Ieyasu, and their rivals—were yet to appear. Kyoto was an open city, the arena of the new elite, and history flowed on undisturbed, ever kind to the prospering *machishu*. They were the new "aristocrats." With the power of their wealth they soon overtook the older ruling class.

Another factor in the postwar situation sealed their success: this was the firm foothold the *machishu* obtained in foreign markets and the tremendous profits that accrued. The port of Sakai, now part of Osaka, saw many ships come and go from Ming China, the Ryukyus, and lands to the south, bringing the merchants immense riches. The Muromachi lords and struggling court nobility were now only nominally in charge. Leaning as they had to upon the financially powerful merchants, the ruling class found its authority diminished with each passing day. The Suminokura family, leader of the banker-

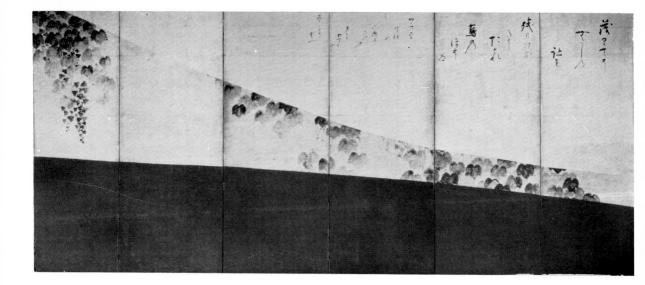

moneylenders; the Chaya family, which monop-
olized foreign trade; and the Goto family of the
gold and silver minting business formed a financial
troika. The Sano, Sawamura, and Osawa were
other leading *machishu* families. Proud gentry, they
preened themselves by building extravagant man-
sions. Many lower-class merchants also enjoyed
great prosperity during the good life of the times.

Naturally, a distinct kind of culture developed,
epitomized by the Gion Festival of Kyoto. This was
the festival of the *machishu*, and the new elite never
showed its power more clearly than when the festival floats paraded through the streets, mastlike
halberds raised high and sides draped in colorful
dyed fabrics imported from the south. The halberds,
symbolizing the masts of trading ships, testified to
the reality of the riches that trade had brought the
machishu.

Some scholars emphasize the fact that this class
sought spiritual support in Nichiren Buddhism.
The Hokke (Lotus Sutra) sect had first spread
through Kyoto in 1294 through the efforts of the
fiery reformer Nichiren's disciple Nichizo. The
sect's doctrine of pragmatic idealism and down-to-

earth benefits, preached in simple terms, appealed
to the Kyoto merchants. Many were converted.
The sect taught that special prayers and rites, called
kajikito, would invoke protection against calamities;
Buddhahood was attainable in this life; and para-
dise was to be realized through the perfecting of
this world. The faith grew still stronger because
of opposition from followers of the Pure Land sect
of Buddhism. With the Hokke uprisings of 1532,
involving the rival sects, the powerful organization
of the *machishu* became fully consolidated.

The leading *machishu* families—the Goto, Chaya,
and Hon'ami—were Nichiren adherents. The
Suminokura clan was also sympathetic. The Kano
family and Hasegawa Tohaku (1539–1610), who
was famous for gold-leaf murals and screen paintings, were also believers; and Sotatsu probably
was, too. How Nichiren Buddhism influenced their
art promises to be a popular subject of forthcoming
studies. In any event, the eminent practicality and
immediacy of the new culture was well suited to the
teachings of Nichiren Buddhism. The struggles of
this sect in history had much in common with those
of the *machishu*.

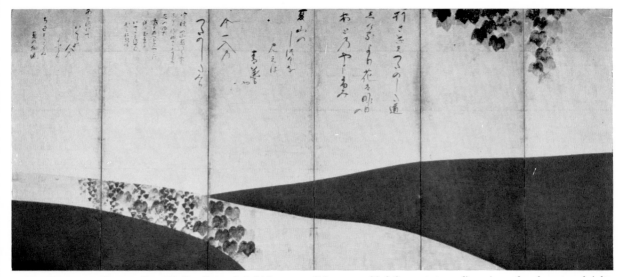

41. *Tawaraya Sotatsu:* Ivy Walk. *Pair of sixfold screens. Colors on gold foil over paper; dimensions of each screen: height, 158.5 cm.; width, 361 cm. Early seventeenth century.*

The nascent culture nurtured many art forms: *sarugaku,* the mimetic dance that influenced Noh; *kusemai,* recitative dancing; *nembutsu odori,* Buddhist dances; Ikenobo's *ikebana* flower arrangements, called *rikka;* the illustrated fairy-tale literature of the popular *otogi-zoshi* books; and the tea cult of Sen no Rikyu, called *wabi chanoyu.* In all, the quiet, elegantly simple medieval culture was changing attire in favor of the gorgeous garb of a freer, more modern day. The *machishu,* not the nobility, were the purveyors of the new culture. And until the war lords once more took over, there was to be a period of grace, thirty or forty years in which the burgeoning new culture would claim the capital, making it come alive with the kind of wide-open activity we associate with our uninhibited culture today.

TOWN PAINTERS AND GENRE PAINTING

The *machi-eshi,* or town painters, were very active in their own cultural segment. Contemporary with them were the famed Kano Motonobu (1476–1559) of the Kano school, whose family was patronized by the Muromachi *bakufu,* and Tosa Mitsunobu (1434–1525)

and his school of painters, who worked for the imperial court. There were many others, too—including Zen priests and military men—who painted.

But the town painters were most numerous. Among them were artists of the Kano and Tosa schools, and also artists set adrift by the breaking up of temple and shrine art bureaus. All these men made their living by doing fairy-tale illustrations, scrolls, fans, screens, furniture decoration, Buddhist paintings, and a multitude of other work. Thus artistic activity kept pace with the growing wealth of the *machishu* and gave birth to what may be called the town-painter style.

Specialists from the Kano and Tosa schools also did decorative paintings for the homes of the merchant elite, but the bulk of this work was produced by the town painters. As artists the latter preferred decorative work. They also found it an excellent export item. The fierce competition for orders meant that only the best would sell. Sales depended on skill, and the work demanded one's fullest efforts. Being beyond the pale of the orthodox schools, the town painters could work very freely, all the more so for the stimulating, uninhibited culture that pre-

42. *Tawaraya Sotatsu: detail of* Life of Priest Saigyo. *Hand scroll. Colors on paper; height, 33.4 cm. 1630. Formerly in the Mori Collection. (See also Figure 15.)*

vailed. They had little liking for the stiff formality of *Kanga*, Chinese-style painting, and the cramped style of the Tosa school held no charm for them, either. Their art soon captivated the old capital.

Town painters produced *hamamatsu* (beach with pines) screens like those in Figures 53 and 57, as well as screens of the "sun and moon landscape" variety, a sample of which can be seen in Figure 43. They turned out countless other works of Momoyama decorative painting. The town painters also made a specialty of genre painting. One notices what is basically a Yamato-e motif in their *hamamatsu* screens, but they have managed to add a *fuzokuga*, or genre-painting, element. Their scrolls and picture-book illustrations were also peopled with figures of their own times. It was only natural that the *machishu*, having come so far through their own efforts, would want to have people like themselves depicted in their art.

This was equally so with the *Rakuchu, Rakugai*

form of painting (Figs. 44, 56). Scenes in and around Kyoto always included the townspeople, who had restored it in the aftermath of the Onin Civil War and who were its real driving force. The inclusion of a Gion scene is sure proof that a genre painting was commissioned by a member of the *machishu*.

The oldest extant *Rakuchu, Rakugai* painting is the screen belonging to the Machida family (Fig. 44). Done by the Tosa school, it depicts the capital as it appeared in the years between 1521 and 1525. A book of *Rakuchu, Rakugai* reproductions in the Tokyo National Museum shows Kyoto between 1543 and 1548. Another screen of the same genre (Fig. 56), in the possession of the Uesugi family, gives us a glimpse of Kyoto between 1548 and 1564; this one was retouched by Kano Eitoku. That these pieces have survived indicates that there were probably many more of the kind. Works like the one done by Eitoku and presented to Uesugi Kenshin (1530–68)

by Oda Nobunaga (1534–82) have come down to us carefully preserved, but the vast majority of the town-painter output has vanished. Still, I do not doubt that much more such work actually existed. I trust the reasoning that finds in town-painter genre painting the inspiration and model for later *Rakuchu, Rakugai* work, if only because there was a wealthy clientele to enjoy it, make presents of it, and shrewdly send it off for export. Eventually Oda Nobunaga and Toyotomi Hideyoshi would officially endorse the Kano school in its *Rakuchu, Rakugai* work, and a stream of Kano genre painting would result. But the groundwork had been laid long before by the town painters and their patrons, the *machishu*.

The new cultural wave was free and exuberant but never loud or garish. A Kyoto tradition going back to the Heian period lent it elegance and refinement. The court connections of the *machishu* also imbued the culture with a distinctively classical atmosphere. The sad tale of a nobility fallen from grace in the late Muromachi period was still a vivid memory. The inner court circle, no longer able to make ends meet, now managed to save face with the help of the upper-class townsmen. This was a blessing for the young *machishu* culture, providing it with court color, making it cherish the past, and prolonging the classical life-style of the nobility. This attachment to the classical was no sudden invention of Koetsu or Sotatsu: it was a general trend that had become increasingly pronounced since late Muromachi times.

THE RISE OF THE MILITARY

Kyoto first encountered the famed general Oda Nobunaga in 1568. He began by issuing currency regulations; he declared collective responsibility for crimes by any citizen, and, just as with the city of Sakai, he set the capital, hitherto self-governed, in a turmoil, forcing it to bow

to military rule. For the *machichu*, the handwriting was on the wall. Nobunaga made his move: he vanquished the shogun, Ashikaga Yoshiaki (1537–97), and destroyed the Muromachi *bakufu* in 1573. Then he concentrated on Kyoto, robbing the wealthy commercial elite of its independence. Despite "protection money" extorted from the *machishu* (thirteen hundred pieces of silver from the citizens of north Kyoto, eight hundred from those of south Kyoto), he left the northern part of the city in flames, alleging that the upper-class *machishu* had been rudely insubordinate. This false imputation was a move of political intimidation, made in order to bring the *machishu* to heel.

At long last a group that had basked in freedom since the Onin Civil War was put under military control. Their autonomy was undermined, and they had to reconcile themselves to seeing their personal wealth stripped away, their Kyoto pride stung all the more by submission to a provincial samurai.

Nobunaga was assassinated in 1582, but there was no letup in military pressure. Nobunaga's successor, Toyotomi Hideyoshi, controlled foreign trade by requiring accreditation of vessels. The merchants recovered financially, but the use of their wealth was restricted. Hideyoshi kept them constantly short with his extravagant expenditures for military unification of the country, castle construction, and the wasteful and fruitless Korean expeditions of 1592 and 1597. There were levies on one thing after another.

Hideyoshi died in 1598. Then, with the battle of Sekigahara in 1600, Tokugawa Ieyasu began to implement his well-laid plans for economic, political, and ideological takeover of the country. His official representative came to look over Kyoto in 1601. By 1603, a ten-man control system was forced on the capital, clamping it completely under Edo rule.

In the Hokoku Shrine in Kyoto, which venerates Hideyoshi, we see the *Hokoku Festival* screens (Fig. 52), depicting the festival held in 1604 to commemorate the death of Hideyoshi. The painting is attributed to Kano Naizen, the younger brother of Eitoku. It shows a scene of unusual excitement. A ring of dancers before the shrine, fifteen hundred people in all, is doing the Hokoku Festival dance of

43. *Sun and moon landscape. Pair of sixfold screens. Colors on gold foil over paper; dimensions of each screen: height, 148 cm.; width, 303.4 cm. C. mid-sixteenth century. Tokyo National Museum.*

August 15 with a strange frenzy. This dance can be interpreted as a demonstration of anger, a display of *machishu* discontent with the military's having usurped their freedom. This theory is strengthened by subsequent events. The Tokugawa shogunate finally quelled the Toyotomi family in the famous winter and summer campaigns of Osaka (1614–15). Ieyasu then promulgated his Laws for Military Houses and enforced other repressive legislation. At this time a frenzied dance called the *furyu odori* spread all over Japan from Ise and Kyoto—an indication of widespread popular resistance to the veil of authority enshrouding the land.

The prohibition of Christianity followed in 1616, and all ships but those of Ming China were restricted to the ports of Nagasaki and Hirado. In 1625 a nationwide system of checking stations was set up. All foreign vessels were excluded in 1633, and in 1635 the daimyo were ordered to attend the shogun's court in Edo every other year. In 1639 isolationist policy prohibited entry of foreigners altogether. The shogunate thus tightened its hold on the merchants and general populace, snatching

their freedoms away one by one. And a feudal system was established that was to shut Japan off from the outside world for two hundred years.

KOETSU AND SOTATSU AMONG THE ELITE

Hon'ami Koetsu was born in 1558, before Nobunaga entered Kyoto and just after the Temmon era (1532–55), when *machishu* culture had reached its zenith. The Hon'ami family home stood on a magnificent site next to the Kanze family residence in northern Kyoto. Like many born into this elite, Koetsu saw and experienced many changes before his death in 1637. The lot of Sotatsu must have been much the same. Both of these great artists knew what it was to live in the slowly tightening vise of Nobunaga, Hideyoshi, and Ieyasu. For the *machishu*, it was a time of inexorable delivery into the hands of a repressive government.

The Hon'ami, Suminokura, and Chaya families were within the cultural orbit of the imperial court circle. Koetsu brushed shoulders with many personages of great standing. There was the dis-

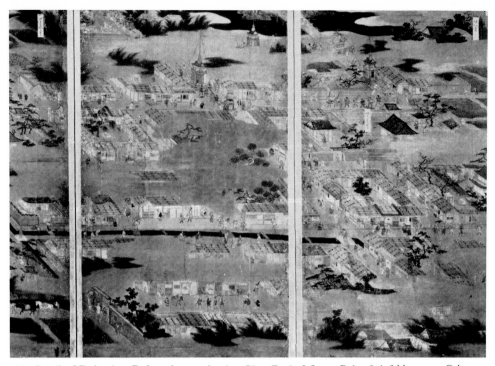

44. *Detail of* Rakuchu, Rakugai *scene showing Gion Festival floats. Pair of sixfold screens. Colors on paper; dimensions of each screen: height, 137.8 cm.; width, 348.4 cm. C. mid-sixteenth century. Machida Collection.*

tinguished Prince Konoe, a man of letters who founded his own school of calligraphy, the Konoe-*ryu;* his son, also an excellent calligrapher, Prince Ozan; the colorful Karasumaru Mitsuhiro, calligrapher and friend of Koetsu; Ichijo Kaneto; Prince Soncho, of Shoren-in temple; the princes Hachijo Toshihito and Hachijo Noritada; and Prince Ryojo, of Manju-in temple. These and many other literati were on hand, and at the center of them all was Emperor Gomizuno-o, who reigned from 1611 to 1629.

The outer fringe of the court also had its cultural figures, such as Haiya Shoeki, whom we have mentioned earlier; Sen no Sotan the tea master; Shokado Shojo, one of the three greatest calligraphers of the times; Raku Donyu, the third Raku pottery master, who tutored his friend Koetsu in ceramics;

Furuta Oribe, another famed tea master; and Oda Urakusai, warrior and tea devotee.

Sotatsu also knew them all. His court connections have come to light recently through the discovery of the Ichijo Kaneto letter (see Figure 132 and page 142). Though a mere town painter, Sotatsu had not come unbidden onto the imperial court scene. He was the companion of Koetsu; he had ties with both *machishu* and court nobles; but most of all, as an artist in traditional Kyoto, the cultural sphere claimed him as one of its own.

Since the military government had been squeezing the life out of the *machishu*, the court of course found itself deeply involved. The maneuvers of the Tokugawa regime, especially its political reshuffling—taking with its right hand what it gave with its left—caused the emperor and his retinue no end

45. *Tawaraya Sotatsu: detail of* Oxen. *Pair of hanging scrolls. Ink on paper; dimensions of each scroll: height, 96.5 cm.; width, 44.3 cm. Early seventeenth century. Chomyo-ji, Kyoto.*

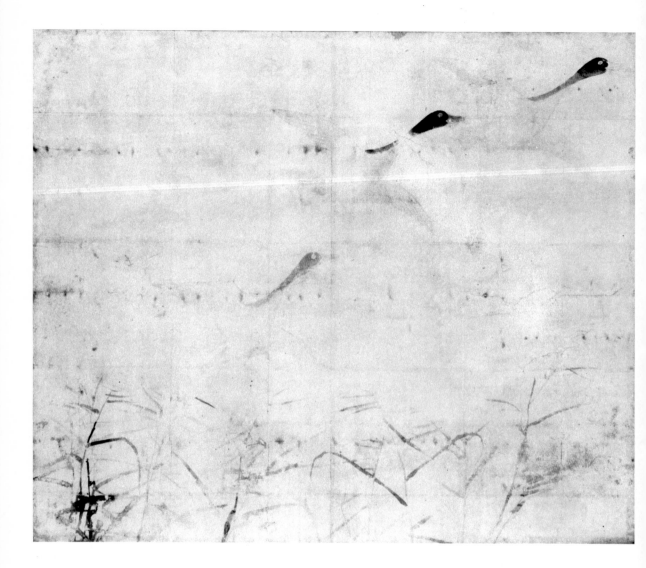

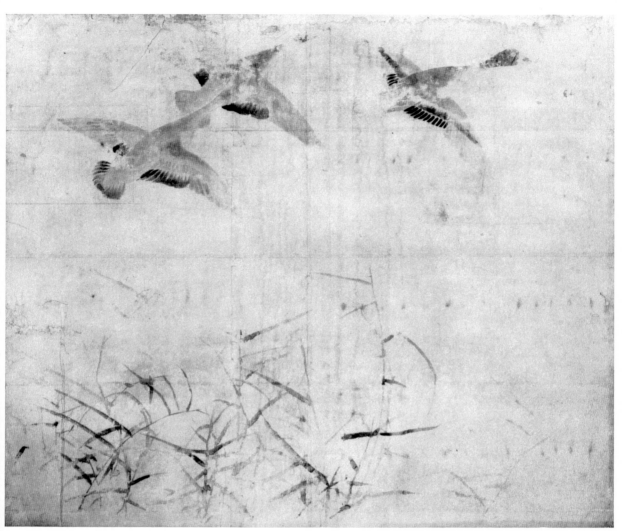

46. *Tawaraya Sotatsu:* Ducks and Reeds. *Pair of single-panel screens. Ink on paper; dimensions of each screen: height, 144.5 cm.; width, 169 cm. Early seventeenth century. Sambo-in, Daigo-ji, Kyoto.*

47. *Tawaraya Sotatsu:* Birds in a Lotus Pond. *Hanging scroll. Ink on paper; height, 118.8 cm.; width, 48.3 cm. Early seventeenth century. Important Cultural Property. Private collection.*

48. *Ogata Kenzan: Camellias. Hanging scroll. Ink on paper; height, 68.5 cm.; width, 24 cm. C. mid-eighteenth century. (See also Figure 154.)*

49. *Ogata Kenzan:* Snake Gourd. *Hanging scroll. Ink on paper; height, 23.5 cm.; width, 33.7 cm. C. mid-eighteenth century.*

50. *Ogata Korin: detail of* Bamboo and Plum. *Pair of twofold screens. Ink on gold foil over paper; dimensions of each screen:* ▷
height, 66.4 cm.; width, 183.2 cm. Early eighteenth century.

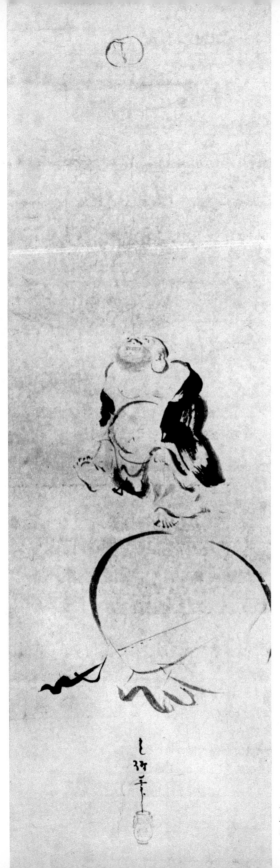

51. *Ogata Korin:* Pu Tai Playing Kickball.
*Hanging scroll. Ink on paper; height, 102.4 cm.;
width, 29.1 cm. Late seventeenth century.*

52. *Detail of* Hokoku Festival. *Pair of sixfold screens. Colors on gold foil over paper; dimensions of each screen: height, 166.9 cm.; width, 362 cm. C. 1604. Hokoku Shrine, Kyoto.*

of suffering. The furor over the "orders incident" in 1629 and the emperor's subsequent abdication brought things to a crisis point. The emperor had ordained four men of Daitoku-ji temple to the priesthood, but the government pronounced the orders invalid. Gomizuno-o was furious, abdicating in favor of Myojo (r. 1630–43), then only a girl of seven. He had been contemplating such a move as far back as the marriage of the second shogun Hidetada's daughter Kazuko into the imperial household. The "orders incident" was the last straw in a long history of military meddling and intrigue. Reinforced in his desire to get away from it all, he retired to a life of seclusion.

A like disenchantment, we may assume, was shared by an anxious court and *machishu*. The court had been spared simply because it was thought to have something to offer the military. The finan-

cially powerful *machishu*, however, were divested of their wealth and effectively ground underfoot. This was a bitter pill for them to swallow: once so free, and long used to a will of their own, they could hardly have been expected simply to suffer in silence.

In the lower *machishu* echelons were those willing to dance to the new tune of the Tokugawa shogunate. They formed what was to be the new merchant class, or *chonin*. They bent to the prevailing wind, taking the lowest rung in the shogunate's warrior-farmer-artisan-merchant caste system, and were thus able to hold onto their wealth. From them sprang the merchants of the later Edo period. The upper-class *machishu*, however, clung to pride in their history and traditions. They would not yield their life-style. How, then, did they show their opposition to the establishment? Through culture

and art. The lower-class *machishu* had performed a brilliant maneuver by cleverly adapting to the times; the upper class would now retreat into the past, preserving and pursuing classical culture and the arts with exceptional enthusiasm.

The culture of the Kan'ei era (1624–44) was formed from this situation. The *machishu* upper and lower classes may have had their differences, but their culture as a whole assumed a posture of resistance. For the upper class and court nobility this meant a pursuit of culture and the arts in keeping with their own dignity and refinement: a resistance sublimated through artistic achievement. Court tastes were to revert to Heian, as seen in the construction of the Katsura Detached Palace and the Shugakuin Detached Palace.

The upper-class *machishu* expressed their nostalgia for the glorious Temmon era, when their culture had flourished, in the Sumiya in Kyoto's Shimabara district, a house of pleasure with paper window paneling of exquisite design (Fig. 58). The *wabi* tea cult, originated by the upper-class *machishu*, was refined by Sen no Sotan (d. 1658). The *rikka* flower art of Ikenobo Senkei was cherished for its magnificent compositions; there was the Gion Festival with the decorative beauty of its floats, supplanting boisterous artistic display with a quest for a more stylized art. All this comprised a form of silent clash with authority on an artistic battlefield with which the opponent was scarcely acquainted. It was the fullest expression of defiance as well as a sophisticated diversion for the Kan'ei *machishu*. If the Kabuki, puppet drama, and a growing pleasure quarter were refinements contributed by the merchants of the lower-class *machishu*, those of the upper class arose from the pursuit of higher culture and arts. And it was the art of the incomparable Koetsu and Sotatsu that was to be its greatest achievement.

It may be going too far to consider the classical revival of Koetsu and Sotatsu a conscious act of resistance. Nevertheless, what fueled their retreat into the past and made them immerse themselves and their creativity so completely therein must have been their search for freedom; it was an almost

53. Hamamatsu *landscape. Pair of sixfold screens. Colors on paper; dimensions of each screen: height, 161 cm.; width, 714 cm. C. mid-sixteenth century.*

automatic resistance to the military government that would deny it. The *machishu* had suffered a severe blow. Was this resistance not a natural reaction, something like a protective scab forming over a wound? Koetsu and Sotatsu were artists born and bred in the tradition of Kyoto culture, and to preserve their integrity was to preserve Kyoto's artistic legacy. Reviving the haunting beauty of Heian, the florescence of classical art, was their means to this end.

This may seem to be escapism. Sotatsu, after all, never depicted in his art the lives of the people who lived about him. And Koetsu avoided the forum also, retreating to Takagamine, devoting himself to dreams of centuries past and trying to revivify them. If they were really against the prevailing powers, why not stand up and be counted? Why did they fail to show their convictions with a real-life portrayal of the people and thus protest against their loss of freedom?

The best way to answer this is simply and quietly to look at their many works. Here is art so rare,

so compellingly beautiful, that it mutes all criticism. Achieving this was their truest form of resistance, and it succeeded better than any other means at hand. No power on earth could ravish this beauty; no force whatever could kill it. It was sweet revenge from the skilled hands of artist "escapists," and also an enterprising way for the *machishu* to make ends meet.

Koetsu did not withdraw to Takagamine in order to retire. Tokugawa Ieyasu gave him the land because he was a representative upper-class *machishu* with good court connections. It was clearly a conciliatory gesture, and Koetsu put it to good use. The popular view that he may have been a Tokugawa spy says something for his cleverness. Koetsu took Tokugawa's offer at face value and, as was his nature, made the most of it.

Had Ieyasu ulterior motives? Koetsu was conveniently situated between court and government, which meant a minimum of mischief and a maximum of the kind of cultural activity essential to peace. A little oil on troubled waters might pull

54. *View of Takagamine, Kyoto.*

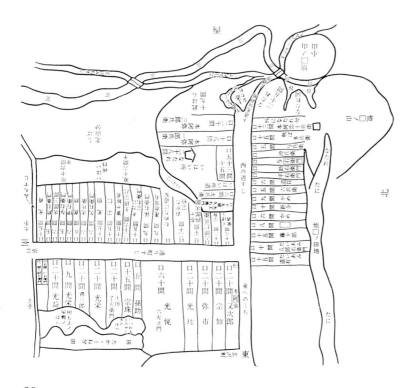

55. *Old map of Takagamine Koetsu Village. The large rectangular area at lower center is Koetsu's residence. Koetsuji, Kyoto.*

56. Kano Eitoku: detail of Rakuchu, Rakugai *scene showing Gion Festival floats. Pair of sixfold screens. Colors on gold foil over paper; dimensions of each screen: height, 159.4 cm.; width, 363.3 cm. C. 1574. Uesugi Collection.*

Kyoto away from political problems. One could always put up with a bit of unpleasant stuffiness from sophisticated quarters like these—I think this was Ieyasu's reasoning and why he could listen to Koetsu without really hearing. "It is a great honor and privilege that his lordship should pay frequent visits to the court. May thy homage continue even into the era of thy son," states the *Hon'ami Family Annals*. Again, we read in the same record: "In those days the great compassion of Kanto favored much our humble selves and family. But here we live and here we shall stay. No command from on high shall make us move to Edo."

The two-edged statement praising the shogun for favoring the imperial court, yet saying that no number of favors received or obligations incurred would make the Hon'ami household remove to Edo, aptly describes Koetsu's delicate situation as he pondered the course of events and juggled relations between court and government. At any rate,

Koetsu accepted the Takagamine land from the shogun with at least the same amount of guile as Ieyasu had in offering it.

Takagamine Koetsu Village was an esthetic stronghold that enabled Koetsu to implement his artistic vision as a whole. His classical renaissance did not begin when he received the land in 1615. It had already been in progress since the beginning of the century. But now he had an ideal place to add the finishing touches. Accompanied by a host of *machishu* of the Nichiren sect, as well as by many artisans and even entire families, he would successfully complete the synthesis of his artistic ideals.

Recent studies of *machishu* adherence to Nichiren Buddhism have resulted in the tendency to emphasize religious factors over esthetic in considering the significance of the Takagamine community. But this only reflects the difference between the historical and artistic points of view, and I too am speaking from my own standpoint in wishing to

place priority on the artistic importance of the village. Here was produced a continuous flow of beautiful works of art: gold lacquer, tea bowls, gold-and-silver painting, and calligraphy. Each work was the incarnation of Koetsu's exquisite sense of beauty.

The cumulative effect of the detached palaces of Katsura and Shugakuin, the Sumiya pleasure house, the Gion Festival, the tea ceremony, *rikka* flower arrangement, theater and dance, and myriad other cultural offspring of the age was like the last brilliant display of fireworks from a culture that had seen its day of glory and now was dying.

Sotatsu did not move out to Takagamine. To keep his place of business accessible he had to remain in town. But he cooperated with Koetsu whenever the occasion called for it, and he cou-

rageously persevered in creating his ideal world. True, his paintings of *monogatari* and floral motifs represented a page out of the past. But it was the immense achievement of Sotatsu's work to shine far brighter than much work dealing with current themes, spanning space and time. We can easily imagine him laughing like his gods of wind and thunder cackling down the skies, as he went about his amazing feat of creating so facilely both a classical revival and a new decorative art form. The free spirit of the *machishu* and the town painter truly came of age in the art of Sotatsu.

It is overly harsh to call Sotatsu's carefully cultivated town-painter style his way of justifying an escape from his times. Had Koetsu and Sotatsu really been "dropping out," joining the court and upper class in esthetic isolation or merely disconso-

57. *Detail of* hamamatsu *landscape. Pair of sixfold screens. Colors on paper; dimensions of each screen: height, 106 cm.; width, 312.6 cm. C. mid-sixteenth century.*

lately drowning their sorrows together in the classics, it is certain that their art could never have attained the heights that it did. No, their isolation was a consciously self-imposed one. They were heirs to the stubborn courage of the *machishu* and the town painters, so indomitable since the Onin Civil War. I personally believe this isolation was their chosen way of tenacious resistance.

If Sotatsu had painted *fuzokuga,* what kind of work would he have been forced to do? The answer tells us precisely why he never took up the form. What met his eyes was the people of an empire forced to grovel before military authority. The merchants, stripped of their freedom, stood lamely on the sidelines. And as we shall see, the people would succumb all too early to the tempation to take the easy way out. The general citizenry and

machishu still had strength to spare for one thing and another, and people who did not have the arts or other cultural pursuits for an option would expend their excess energy on pleasure.

Needless to say, motifs of this sort were not for Sotatsu, much less Koetsu. Decadent beauty held no attraction for them. What held Sotatsu's attention far more than anything he actually saw around him was the beguiling beauty and charm of classical art. This was an undying beauty, and Sotatsu felt his artistic sensibilities come alive in contact with it. The decadent and the classical were quite incompatible for him.

This is why there was no place in Sotatsu's world for genre painting. Instead, he devoted himself to constantly refining the *monogatari,* floral, and landscape painting forms. He kept to his course un-

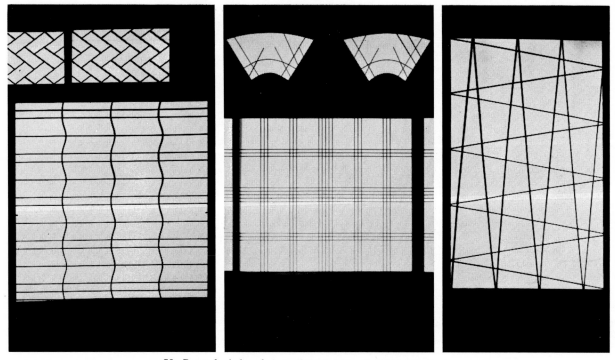

58. Papered-window designs of the Sumiya. C. 1670–80. Kyoto.

swervingly; he had none of the nervous or fickle tastes of the dilettante. And the more subtly he refined these forms, the more his ability grew—a fact no one knew better than Koetsu.

It is said that Sotatsu was a painter of happy things. One certainly senses a richness and balance in his works. But once he is placed within the context of his times, even his happier scenes evince more than a little shadow. Look, for example, at the people in his *Genji* and *Ise* paintings: the tense figures and facial expressions seem to express the mind of Sotatsu himself. Or take a closer look at the faces of his gods of wind and thunder as they tumble the heavens: they have a repressed look, as of something held back. I think that Sotatsu could only feel completely at ease when painting flowers.

CHAPTER FIVE

A Society in Transition

THE DYING ELITE Koetsu passed away in 1637 at his cottage in Takagamine, the Taikyo-an. We cannot be sure when Sotatsu died, but since his successor, Sosetsu, received the title of *hokkyo* in 1642, it is reasonable to assume that Sotatsu had died before that. Suminokura Soan, who had been close to both, had died earlier, in 1632; and Karasumaru Mitsuhiro had followed in 1638. The group of upper-class *machishu* and court nobles surrounding Koetsu had slipped away one by one. A generation that had personally experienced the decline of the Kyoto *machishu* under the threefold rule of Nobunaga, Hideyoshi, and Ieyasu was dying. A new generation of a different type, raised under the shogunate and accustomed to Edo rule, had grown up in its place.

All this makes it difficult to assign an exact place to the art of Koetsu and Sotatsu. That their work ranks among the greatest achievements of Japanese art goes without saying. But besides being a culmination, their art was also a beginning. Considered in the light of the art of the *machishu* and court following the Onin Civil War, it was indeed a culmination; but seen from Kan'ei onward, it was the start of a new decorative art form. Social commentators are prone to take Koetsu and Sotatsu to task for the passivity of their work, calling it an escape from harsh realities. But this is only a superficial judgment. History has vindicated them and the positive side of their art. The proof of this is the art of Korin and Kenzan, their spiritual heirs.

PEACE UNDER THE MILITARY The half-century between the Kan'ei and Genroku eras brought political stability to the land under Edo rule. With the Shimabara revolt of 1638, the Christians were completely quelled and the peasant revolts put down. In 1651 there was a single instance of social unrest when Yui Shosetsu, a prominent samurai, was implicated in a plot against the shogun and arrested. He committed suicide, and the incipient revolt against the government ended.

Power passed undiminished from the third Tokugawa shogun, Iemitsu (1603–51), to Ietsuna, his eldest son (1639–80), then to Tsunayoshi, his fourth son (1646–1709). The military had the country well in hand and carefully cut off from foreign influence. It was a hothouse in which peace could be preserved artificially. All of Japan, the ruling classes included, was forced into the warrior-farmer-artisan-merchant mold. This was a caste system of stereotypes, with life rigidly ruled by the Confucian ethic. The contrived atmosphere only intensified as time passed, and the long calm made for a spineless people.

Kan'ei culture's longstanding friction with feudalism was forgotten, and the court came to take life under the military for granted; the *machishu* and townspeople, feeling they owed the peace to the authorities, and with most of their old resentment gone, dedicated themselves to the dubious task of bringing Kan'ei's immature pleasures to full-blown

59 (above, left). Yuzen-zome *kimono. Dyed design on red figured* satin. Early eighteenth century. Yuzenshi-kai, Kyoto.

60 (above, right). Kaigetsudo Ando: Courtesan and Attendant. *Hanging scroll. Colors on paper; height, 98.2 cm.; width, 44.6 cm. Early eighteenth century.*

61. Yuzen-zome *kimono. Dyed design on crepe. Early eighteenth century. Nagao Art Museum, Tokyo.*

62. *Detail of* Women at Play. *Pair of fourfold screens. Colors on gold foil over paper; dimensions of each screen: height, 86.5 cm.; width, 219.4 cm. C. mid-seventeenth century.*

flower. Even Koetsu's words were forgotten: in 1697 his great-grandson Kotsu gave the Takagamine property back to the Tokugawa shogunate, then moved to Edo.

THE EVOLUTION OF GENRE PAINTING

An early indication of the way the tide was turning appeared in genre art. While Koetsu and Sotatsu had avoided it in favor of neo-classicism, the surrounding lower-class *machishu* and general public found its themes very much to their liking. Many of these paintings remain, attesting to the form's popularity in post-Kan'ei times. The Tokyo National Museum has a number of Kyoto genre-painting screens. There are two sets of Shijo riverbed screens, one owned by Shiro Domoto of Kyoto and the other, shown in Figure 85, in the Seikado in Tokyo; the So'o-ji temple screens in the Tokugawa Reimei-kai, Tokyo; the *Dancing Women* screens (Fig. 66) in the Kyoto Municipal Art Museum; the *Yuna* (Bathhouse Girls) screens (Fig. 63) in the Atami Art Museum; and other works, such as the *Kabuki-zoshi* scroll and the *Women at Play* screens of Figure 62. The subject matter and general attitude found in these genre pieces signal a definite transition along with the evolving culture. We see a gradual drift from genre depicting the general public to a more limited form showing the world of pleasure. This depiction becomes increasingly decadent with the passage of time.

Amusement has always been an important part

63. Yuna *(Bathhouse Girls)*. *Hanging scroll. Colors on paper; height, 72.6 cm.; width, 80.3 cm. Early seventeenth century. Atami Art Museum, Shizuoka Prefecture.*

of life, and paintings of such themes are easy enough to like. But to avoid depicting life as it really is in favor of its pleasurable aspects alone can justly be called the beginning of cultural distortion. Genre painting not only shows a bent for theatrical entertainment and the pleasure quarters but also allows us a look at the sensuous side of daily social life. The wealthy townsmen, bereft of freedom and frustrated in being unable to trade overseas, surely sought here an outlet for pent-up energies. A society at peace is all too willing to afford such release. The upper-class merchants still had time and energy to spare, and the general run of the people were willing enough to enjoy peace by wallowing in pleasure. The rush to the theaters and pleasure quarters, like a torrent unleashed, is vividly recorded for us in genre art, recalling the manners and morals that

we know so well from post–World War II Japan.

In accenting the sensuous and the seamy, genre painting naturally degenerated into eroticism. The taste in amusements among the townspeople grew ever more wanton; a world of pleasure flourished, built on power and money. It was inevitable that a sensual culture like this should produce the *ukiyo-e* form, through a process in which genre painting became pleasure painting, then evolved into *ukiyo-e*. The transition itself reflects in miniature the change in social conditions from the Kan'ei to the Genroku era.

GENROKU CULTURE   What was Kyoto like in Genroku times? A Dutch doctor has recorded his impressions of the capital in 1691: "Kyoto is the center of Japan's various arts,

64. *Detail of* The Story of Honda Heihachiro. *Pair of twofold screens. Colors on paper; dimensions of each screen: height, 72.7 cm.; width, 78.8 cm. Early seventeenth century. Tokugawa Art Museum, Nagoya.*

production, and business. There are copper refining, minting, and printing. Brocades, gorgeous dyed fabrics, exquisite carvings, musical instruments, lacquerware, and magnificent paintings are produced and sold. Kyoto also specializes in copperware, swordcraft, luxurious clothing, ornaments, and toys. These products are famous throughout the land; made in the capital, they are prized by all."

All this meant great prosperity. The people of Kyoto lived the "good life." About this time wadded-silk garments became standard clothing, and women were beautifully clad in sumptuous long-sleeved kimono. This spurred the textile industry, and it was the high point for the famed Nishijin fabrics of Kyoto. The array of products was amazing; the gorgeous colors and exquisiteness

of Genroku patterns made this the most dazzling era in the history of Japanese clothing. The ultimate in printed-silk dyeing techniques, the *Yuzenzome* (starch-resist dyeing) process (Figs. 59, 61) was also perfected. From what we can gather, the *fuzoku,* or "manners and customs," of Kyoto were of an elegance beyond imagining.

Diet developed along with dress. First came the staples, then the side courses, followed by all kinds of sweets, which we now know under the name of "Kyoto *meika.*" Restaurants began to proliferate at this time, too. Living accommodations improved: the use of *tatami* straw-mat flooring and *futon* quilts for bedding became general. Furniture makers flourished, and decorative techniques improved. Luxury items were so common as to invite frequent sumptuary edicts from the shogunate.

The first popular novels were also written in the Genroku era. Ihara Saikaku wrote his *ukiyo-zoshi,* or "tales of the floating world." This type of writing, frankly dealing with merchants, their bourgeois lives and pleasures, money and women, would have been inconceivable before Genroku. Another product of popular culture, the *haikai,* a seventeen-syllable verse form that preceded the haiku, also made its debut at about this time. The illustrious poet Matsuo Basho, using this form, raised the ordinary stuff of daily life to a new cultural height in his verse. *Haikai* permeated the life of the people: anyone could turn out a verse or two, an unprecedented phenomenon largely owing to the liberal spirit of Genroku times.

The people of the day sought amusement at the theater and in the pleasure quarters. Genroku theater began with the Kamigata puppet theater of Kyoto; this led to the ballad-drama form called *gidayu-bushi,* originated by Takemoto Gidayu (1651–1714), the famed Osaka storyteller and musician. Puppet plays drew enthusiastic audiences. The

playwright Chikamatsu Monzaemon (1653–1724) perfected both Kabuki and puppet plays as theater. Kabuki advanced from dance to drama, the proliferation of plays and troupes and technical improvements in staging winning it ever-increasing popularity. Great Kabuki actors like Sakata Tojuro and Yoshizawa Ayame appeared, and the art of actors specializing in female roles also began to develop.

The major pleasure quarters were the Shimabara, Gion, and Fushimi districts of Kyoto. They have been described as "dens of iniquity," but they were actually havens of equity and freedom in an otherwise restricted, feudalistic society. Here the townsmen, their energies otherwise suppressed, could find solace and diversion. Here a culture committed to pleasure was cultivated.

In Edo *ukiyo-e* prints continued to develop. The Genroku era saw the evolution from *sumizuri-e,* monochrome prints, to *tan-e,* early color prints, and *urushi-e,* "lacquer paintings." Kyoto followed suit, fostering decadent tastes with erotic depictions of

65. Women's Entertainments. *Pair of sixfold screens. Colors on gold foil over paper; dimensions of each screen: height, 153 cm.; width, 363 cm. C. mid-seventeenth century. Yamato Bunkakan, Nara.*

actors and beautiful women. Going to the theater, dropping into the pleasure quarters and the tea-houses along the Shijo River—Genroku life was surely akin to that of present-day Tokyo. The luxurious teahouses had walls lined with silk, velvet-covered floors, and goldfish swimming in crystal ceilings. Beautiful women were in waiting behind glass panels, ready with rare foods to tempt the palate.

Of a healthier stripe were such merchant amusements as Noh plays, tea ceremony, and flower arrangement. The Ikenobo style of flower arrangement, together with the tea cult, spread to the general populace. The three sons of Sen no Sotan opened their own schools of tea, developing the famous *sado* tea ceremony of the shogunate. Upper-class merchants began collecting famous tea utensils and turned tea-cultist. Wealthy merchants like Konoike Sotei and Yamanaka Do'oku spent fortunes on tea utensils, putting *chanoyu* at the top of the list of townsman amusements. Until Genroku, teaching tea ceremony had not been a profession.

Along with tea, Noh became a leading merchant pastime. The government gave it official sanction, but it spread beyond the military elite in Genroku times to permeate the general public. Its measured chants became a popular everyday amusement: "Noh is the fashion with most of the lords. Even retainers, merchants, and peasants enjoy it. Everyone is chanting or playing instruments from dawn to dusk," states a contemporary account. It was evidently popular to the point of being obnoxious: "In times of peace, 'the bow is in its case and the sword in its scabbard' indeed. Ah, peace!"

THE WORLD OF KORIN AND KENZAN

This was the world into which came the Ogata brothers. Korin was born in 1658, Kenzan in 1663. A culture coming to its fullest bloom would nourish them and their art. In 1688, the first year of the Genroku era, Korin had turned thirty and Kenzan, twenty-five; their art was just beginning to flower when Genroku got under way.

66. *Detail of* Dancing Women. *Pair of sixfold screens. Colors on gold foil over paper; dimensions of each screen: height, 63.2 cm.; width, 245.8 cm. Early seventeenth century. Kyoto Municipal Art Museum.*

The father of Korin and Kenzan ran a prosperous dry-goods establishment called the Kariganeya. In tracing its history we note close family ties with the Hon'ami family. The brothers' great-grandfather Ogata Dohaku had married Hon'ami Koetsu's sister and was said to be a retainer of Asai Nagamasa (1545–73), a prominent daimyo. Nagamasa's daughter Yodogimi became the mistress of Toyotomi Hideyoshi.

The business was started by Dohaku's son Sohaku (1570–1631) when Nagamasa's youngest daughter was married to Tokugawa Hidetada. Sohaku probably began by simply purveying, then gradually became a full-blown merchant as time passed. Hidetada's wife would receive clothing orders from her older sister Yodogimi and pass them on. The young business turned a fine profit and was officially named the Kariganeya.

When Hidetada became the second Tokugawa shogun, the Kariganeya became the official purveyor to the government, catering to the wives of nobles. And later, when Hidetada's daughter Kazuko married Emperor Gomizuno-o, the Kariganeya became court dressmaker by appointment to the empress, now Tofukumon-in.

Thus the Ogata family established a good business foundation in Kyoto. Of the upper-class *machishu* like the Hon'ami family, the Ogata continued to prosper. That Sohaku had a mansion in Takagamine Koetsu Village indicates connections between the two families. The Ogata brothers thus were firmly ensconced in the upper level of the *machishu* and within the court cultural circle, enjoying the same artistic environment that Koetsu and Sotatsu had. It was natural, even inevitable, that Korin and Kenzan should emulate them.

67. *Tawaraya Sotatsu: detail of* Bugaku. *Pair of twofold screens. Colors on gold foil over paper; dimensions of each screen:* ▷ *height, 155 cm.; width, 169 cm. Early seventeenth century. Sambo-in, Daigo-ji, Kyoto. (See also Figure 7.)*

68. *Hon'ami Koetsu and Tawaraya Sotatsu: detail of* Thousand Cranes. *Hand scroll with painting by Sotatsu and calligraphy by Koetsu. Gold-and-silver underpainting on paper; height, 34.1 cm.; length, 1,460 cm. Early seventeenth century. (See also Figure 124.)*

69. *Ogata Korin:* Thousand Cranes. *Incense wrapper mounted on a hanging scroll. Gold-and-silver underpainting on silk; height, 33.2 cm.; width, 24.6 cm. Early eighteenth century.*

70. *Ogata Korin:* Red and White Plum Blossoms. *Pair of twofold screens. Colors on gold foil and silver foil over paper; dimensions of each screen: height, 106 cm.; width, 172 cm. Early eighteenth century. Atami Art Museum, Shizuoka Prefecture. (See also Figure 71.)*

71. Ogata Korin: detail of Red and White Plum Blossoms. *Pair of twofold screens. Colors on gold foil and silver foil over paper; dimensions of each screen: height, 106 cm.; width, 172 cm. Early eighteenth century. Atami Art Museum, Shizuoka Prefecture. (See also Figure 70.)*

72. *Ogata Korin and Ogata Kenzan: square dish by Kenzan with bamboo painting and calligraphy by Korin. Rust painting;*
length, 21.7 cm.; width, 21.8 cm. Early eighteenth century. Fujita Art Museum, Osaka.

73. *Ogata Korin:* Irises. *Pair of sixfold screens. Colors on gold foil over paper; dimensions of each screen: height, 151.2 cm.; width, 360.7 cm. Early eighteenth century. Nezu Art Museum, Tokyo.*

74. *Ogata Korin: detail of* Waves. *Pair of twofold screens. Colors on gold foil over paper; dimensions of each screen: height, 146.6 cm.; width, 165.4 cm. Early eighteenth century. Metropolitan Museum of Art, New York.*

75. *Ogata Korin:* Tatsutagawa. *Round fan mounted on a hanging scroll. Colors on paper; height, 24.6 cm.; width, 24.4 cm. ▷ Early eighteenth century. Goto Art Museum, Tokyo.*

76. *Ogata Korin: detail of* Flowers and Grasses. *Hand scroll mounted in frames. Colors on paper; dimensions of each section: height, 36 cm.; width, 131 cm. 1705. (See also Figure 90.)*

77. *Ogata Korin: Fuyuki kosode. Colors on white satin; length, 150 cm.; width at shoulders, 43.3 cm. Early eighteenth century.* ▷
Tokyo National Museum.

78. Ogata Kōrin: detail of box decorated with fan paintings. Colors on paper over gold lacquer; length, 38.2 cm.; width, 27.5 cm.; height, 19 cm. Early eighteenth century. Yamato Bunkakan, Nara. (See also Figure 99.)

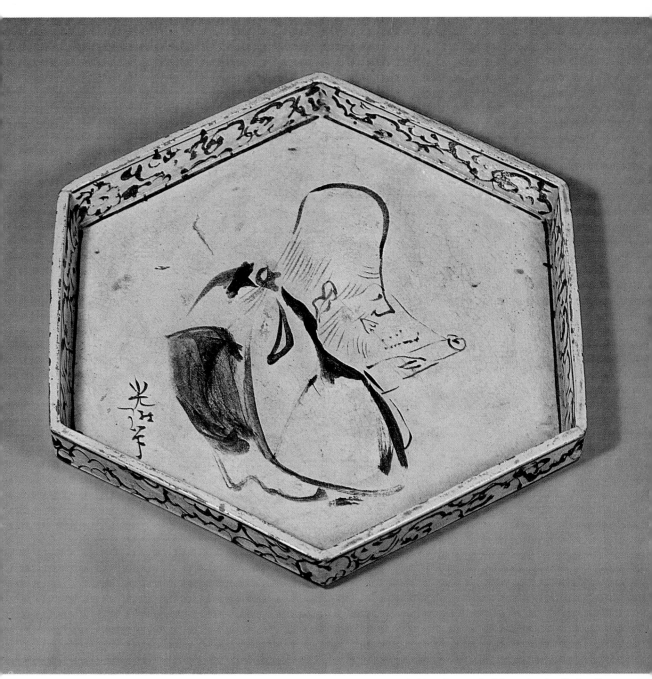

79. *Ogata Korin and Ogata Kenzan: hexagonal dish by Kenzan with painting of Shou Lao, god of longevity, by Korin. Rust painting; length, 27.1 cm.; width, 24 cm.; height, 2.8 cm. Early eighteenth century. Okura Cultural Foundation, Tokyo.*

80. Ogata Kenzan: "Waterfall" tea bowl. Rust painting; diameter, 10.3 cm. Early eighteenth century. (See also Figure 150.)

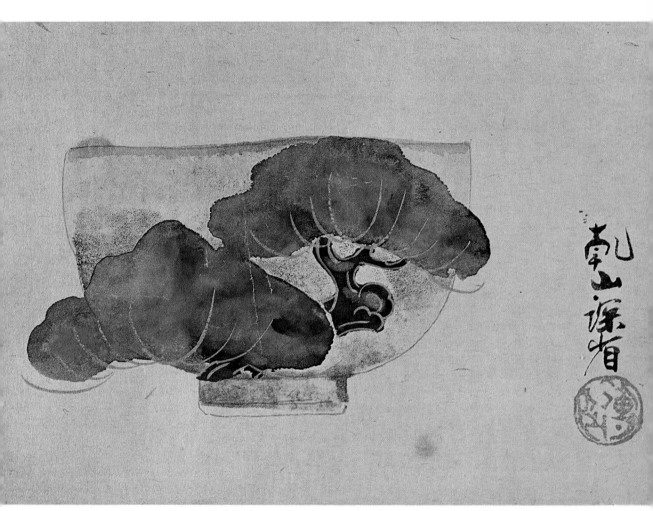

81. *Ogata Kenzan:* Pine on Tea Bowl. *Hanging scroll. Colors on paper; height, 14.4 cm.; width, 22.5 cm. Early eighteenth century.*

83. *Ogata Kenzan: bowl with painting of red and white plum blossoms. Diameter, 20.2 cm. 1737. (See also Figure 151.)*

◁ 82. *Ogata Kenzan: square dish with painting of camellias. Length, 23 cm.; width, 23 cm.; height, 12.3 cm. 1737.*

84. *Ogata Kenzan: square dish with painting of lotuses. Rust painting; length, 24 cm.; width, 24 cm.; height, 2.8 cm. 1737.*

85. Detail of Shijo riverbed scene. Pair of twofold screens. Colors on gold foil over paper; dimensions of each screen: height, 164.3 cm.; width, 172 cm. C. 1620. Seikado, Tokyo.

But Korin and Kenzan were born to a different world. The *machishu* had changed; almost all those of the true upper-class mold like the Hon'ami family had disappeared. The Ogata clan was just barely of the same order but shared the same precarious lot of the has-beens, this because its position as privileged purveyor to the court was in peril. The loss of its single customer would be fatal unless it could come up with a new clientele, involving a complete revamping of its business approach. Empress Tofukumon-in died in 1678, leaving the Kariganeya in serious financial straits. The family had lost money in making loans to daimyo; a switch to the merchant market failed, and finally bankruptcy ensued. Korin and Kenzan found themselves growing up just as the upper-class *machishu* elite was crumbling.

After Sohaku, the founder of the Kariganeya, came his son Soken (1623–87). He inherited the family business and was the father of Kenzan and Korin. A student of the Koetsu school of calligraphy and the Kano school of painting, he was widely read and was well versed in the tea ceremony. He appears to have been a sophisticated man of considerable culture. Soken's business acumen, however, apparently left much to be desired. It would seem that he did not have the adaptability required for the fast-changing business world. Still, he provided his two sons with sufficient wealth, and they had a happy youth indeed.

Soken bequeathed the family business to his oldest son, Tosaburo. The younger sons, Korin and Kenzan, received their fair share of money, land, and goods. Soken's legacy to his sons, we read, also included a set of Noh instruments for Korin, and for Kenzan a writing box and a hanging scroll by the famous Chinese Zen calligrapher Yin Yueh-chiang. These gifts reflect the way in which he viewed his sons: Korin the playful, Kenzan the studious. We will see the same qualities in their art.

CHAPTER SIX

The Life and Art of Korin

KORIN'S YOUTH As a youth Korin studied painting under Yamamoto Soken of the Kano school. He never planned to make a career of art. It was his having exhausted the paternal legacy and being faced with the Kariganeya's bankruptcy that changed his mind. Until this happened he had only been dabbling in painting techniques. He was obviously talented, so textile-design aspects of the family business (Fig. 148) intrigued him; he probably created original patterns, though always as an amateur. What the designs were able to do, however, was give him an attachment to Sotatsu and Sosetsu, and his later painting would be profoundly influenced by them.

Life was carefree for the young Korin. He had no responsibility in the family business and, with money to spare, could spend his time in the pleasure districts. I would venture to say that his was the life of a typical pleasure-loving libertine. He had many love affairs, took part in the Nijo family's salon, and showed himself witty and urbane; in all, he posed as a Genroku dandy.

These youthful days of profligacy were to shape his art in important ways. The elegant sophistication of his painting style and his keen perception would owe much in polish to the world of easy grace in which he moved. His tastes caused him to look down his nose at the *nouveaux riches,* and this helped give his art its peculiar dark twist. We must recognize that Korin's youthful dissipations did not represent a mere squandering of his birthright.

The house of cards had to collapse. In about 1693 it became apparent that the money loaned to daimyo could not be recovered, and Korin had to borrow money from his younger brother, Kenzan. Next he was forced to sell the property his father had willed him. And finally he had to strike out on his own and earn a living. It happened that Kenzan had often contemplated the same, hoping to live by making and selling pottery. So Korin helped by painting designs on Kenzan's pottery. In 1699 they fired their kiln and together somehow managed to make ends meet.

It was probably at about this time that Korin decided to be a painter. He received the title of *hokkyo* as early as 1701, so there must have been a considerable interval before that in which he was able to perfect his technique. Working for a living must have been difficult for the fun-loving playboy in Korin. Sheer need had forced him to put face and honor second. Still, he swallowed his pride and, with art as a profession, made of the mortification a steppingstone to artistic achievement.

KORIN'S ART *Pu Tai Playing Kickball* (Fig. 51) is an example of Korin's pre-*hokkyo* work. The brushwork is individualistic, departing from the Kano style. The feeling is also quite removed from Zen treatment. A clownish Pu Tai, god of fortune, kicking a ball into the air—this displays both Korin's brilliant brush and his wry attitude toward public opinion; it shows an iconoclastic

86 (left). Ogata Korin and Ogata Kenzan: square dish by Kenzan with painting by Korin of the poet Huang Shan-ku watching sea gulls. Rust painting; length, 22 cm.; width, 22.1 cm.; height, 3 cm. Early eighteenth century. Tokyo National Museum. (See also Figure 107.)

87 (right). Ogata Korin and Ogata Kenzan: square dish by Kenzan with painting by Korin of waves and plovers. Rust painting; length, 22.1 cm.; width, 22.1 cm.; height, 2.7 cm. C. 1699.

kind of irony and wit. The meaning of this kind of expression, as we shall see, is deeply bound up with the essence of Korin the man. But before dwelling further on this, we should get a broader picture of Korin's art.

Korin's many ink paintings can be divided into two categories: those with a bold stroke and sharp line similar to the work of the painter Kaiho Yusho (1533–1615), and those with the peculiar dark twist mentioned above. Typical of the former are the *Bamboo and Plum* screens (Fig. 50), while the *Pu Tai Playing Kickball* and *Vimalakirti* (Fig. 89) hanging scrolls fall into the latter group.

The same categories hold for Korin's pottery painting, which can also be considered *suibokuga*. Painting on pottery differs from painting on silk or paper in that one deals in glaze, shape, and texture and has the limitations of space, rough surface, and glazing to contend with. It is no easy field, and these factors contrive to accentuate an artist's abilities and quality. Korin appears to have delighted in the challenges of the medium and even to have taken satisfaction from them. His crane, plum, and bamboo paintings on pottery (Fig. 72) have a sharp, ambitious stroke; the six-sided dish depicting Shou Lao, god of longevity (Fig. 79), and the square dish with Shih-te, a Zen hermit of China (Fig. 3), display his unique touch.

The distinctive style of Korin, which led to his being honored as the originator of the style known as Rimpa (literally, Korin school), is seen in his gorgeous flowers-and-grasses painting. While his ink painting shows only his individuality, the larger floral paintings in the tradition of Sotatsu place him at the summit of another medium, that of decorative art.

88. *Ogata Korin: detail of* Cranes. *Pair of fourfold screens. Ink and light colors on paper; dimensions of each screen: height, 150 cm.; width, 240 cm. Late seventeenth century.*

Floral-theme painting had become familiar to all through Sosetsu and the Tawaraya atelier after Sotatsu's death. Gold-and-silver painting and screen painting, both based on the Sotatsu style, not only were acclaimed among the court and moneyed classes but became a widespread form of decorative painting, thanks to the tremendous output of the Tawaraya. There is evidence that in later years Sosetsu even traveled to Kanazawa, on the Japan Sea coast, to make screens with floral themes fashionable there.

The painters who followed saw a need to systematize the decorative patterns in the floral genre. Instead of the warm, friendly flower forms so natural to Sotatsu, there was a catering to the untrained eye, aiming to draw attention by flamboyance. Sosetsu was extremely adept at scattering brilliant patterns over a surface. Later, in the Genroku era,

Korin came to know these patterns through his design work at the Kariganeya.

KORIN AND SOTATSU Korin had a deep respect for Sotatsu and often reproduced his work meticulously. This is evident from Korin's *Matsushima* screens, his *Flowers and Grasses* scroll (Figs. 76, 90), and his *God of Wind and God of Thunder* screens. Korin was nevertheless a man of his own day, a Genroku artist. He was a different kind of person from Sotatsu and in addition would naturally have felt some rivalry with his senior of Kan'ei times. This feeling was reinforced by confidence in his own perceptions and techniques, and he had the kind of temperament that had to express itself. In Sotatsu's flower painting he probably saw an old-fashioned naturalism. Here we see in Korin not so much the leader of the

89. *Ogata Korin:* Vimalakirti. *Hanging scroll. Ink on paper; height, 37.8 cm.; width, 54.5 cm. Early eighteenth century.*

latest Genroku fashion as the pioneer of a new style in art. But examining his reproductions of Sotatsu's *Matsushima* and *God of Wind and God of Thunder* screens we begin to realize how unable Korin was to keep Sotatsu from impinging upon his awareness.

Korin's *Irises* screens (Fig. 73) and *Red and White Plum Blossoms* screens (Figs. 70, 71) have the composition and color principle of decorative painting, but they reject a sentimental treatment in favor of sweep and overall effect. They unite color, form, and perspective, but otherwise the expression of the flowers themselves is renounced for Korin's personal, decorative conception of a painting surface. The treatment is cold, compared to the warm floral expression of Sotatsu. But burning coolly in the background we feel Korin's rigorous decorative sense and his jousting with the specter of Sotatsu.

Korin, like Sotatsu, painted fan surfaces. Representative are the fan paintings affixed to a box (Figs. 78, 99), which come down to us together with the Korin-like novelty of the idea itself. Unable to overcome Sotatsu in composition, Korin counts on bright colors to make his point. The fans we see on the box present a beautiful Genroku symphony of color.

In contrast to Sotatsu's folding-fan compositional method, which we discussed earlier, Korin's painting is marked by round-fan composition (Figs. 94, 95). This derived from his long hours of design work at the Kariganeya, where he nearly always handled his subject within a circle. Korin's compositional sense in arranging plum blossoms, autumn grasses (Fig. 143), the *yatsuhashi* (eight-plank bridge), and maples (Fig. 75) on round fans rivals that of Sotatsu.

90. Ogata Korin: Flowers and Grasses. *Hand scroll mounted in frames. Colors on paper; dimensions of each section: height, 36 cm.; width, 131 cm. 1705. (See also Figure 76.)*

91 (above). Ogata Korin: "Suminoe" writing box. Gold lacquer; length, 24.5 cm.; width, 23.1 cm.; height, 9.5 cm. Early eighteenth century. Seikado, Tokyo.

92 (right). Ogata Korin: portrait of Nakamura Kuranosuke. Hanging scroll. Colors on silk; height, 109.1 cm.; width, 46.1 cm. 1704. Yamato Bunkakan, Nara.

93. *Ogata Korin: detail of* T'ai Kung-wang Fishing. *Pair of twofold screens. Colors on paper; dimensions of each screen: height, 166.4 cm.; width, 180.7 cm. Early eighteenth century.*

His methods in *monogatari* pieces and paintings of people were preceded by those of Sotatsu. The latter had relied more on surface composition than message as a method; Korin would make his own method a way of explicating literary content. Unfortunately, his means did not match his materials, and this tells us why much of Korin's *monogatari* and figure work falls short of being great art. It is the peculiar dark twist in these works, discussed earlier, that instead commands attention.

KORIN'S DARK SIDE With this overview of Korin's art, a few salient characteristics of his work begin to emerge. His rigorous, sharp decorative painting of flowers is distinctive. The beauty of Korin's achievement,

just as he intended, ranks it with that of Sotatsu, and he too is a model of what is basic in Japanese art. His *Red and White Plum Blossoms* and *Irises* screens compare with Sotatsu's *Bugaku* and *God of Wind and God of Thunder* screens as masterpieces of decorative painting. They go beyond distilling for us the quintessence of Genroku to present us with what is Japanese in Japanese art. Korin, with Sotatsu in mind and ever bent on outdoing him, achieved all this with his work. He possessed a brilliant talent—sharp, stylish, and unconventional; and these pieces show him at his best. What I would like to draw attention to, however, is not Korin's more obvious and comfortable aspects but his less-known, darker side.

We saw this earlier in connection with *Pu Tai*

94 (above). Ogata Korin: round fan with painting of bamboo. Ink on paper; height, 24.5 cm.; width, 24.3 cm. Early eighteenth century.

95 (right). Ogata Korin: round fan with painting of irises. Colors on paper; height, 23.6 cm.; width, 24.2 cm. Early eighteenth century.

Playing Kickball and in some other ink paintings: an indefinable peculiarity of expression that is hard to dismiss simply as sarcasm or puckish humor; it is a certain feeling of repugnance toward things, a cynicism, a vein of snobbery bordering on contempt. We see it in his *Vimalakirti*, and again in *T'ai Kung-wang Fishing* (Fig. 93). It is this kind of work, I think, that mirrors the true mind and heart of Korin.

I FIND IT excessive to conjecture, as has been done, that Korin was involved in a counterfeit-money plot through his connection with Nakamura Kuranosuke (Fig. 92), an official of the Kyoto mint. Korin was a fun-loving playboy and fond of dalliance, but he can hardly be accused of criminal

conspiracy. No, with Korin what is dark is not connected with his outward personality or activities; the shadow is of his substance.

One interpretation finds the roots of this dark side in the unsettled nature of his life. Korin, goes the argument, seemed unrepentant after squandering his father's legacy; he continued to live from hand to mouth, as is proved by promissory notes and pawn tickets. After his patron, Nakamura Kuranosuke, was found guilty of counterfeiting money and banished, Korin was apparently aided by the Fuyuki family, rich timber merchants of Edo, but not to the extent of allowing him to live on the extravagant scale of his youth. An artist's income in the Genroku era was very low in comparison with today. This continual scratching for a

96. *Ogata Korin:* Sekiya. *Sketch.*
Ink on paper. Late seventeenth cen-
tury. Osaka Municipal Art Museum.

97. *Ogata Korin:* Pu Tai Crossing
a River. *Sketch. Ink on paper. Late*
seventeenth century. Osaka Municipal
Art Museum.

98. *Letter by Ogata Korin. Height, 31.6 cm.; width, 105.5 cm. 1709. Yamato Bunkakan, Nara.*

99. Ogata Korin: box decorated with fan paintings. Colors on paper over gold lacquer; length, 38.2 cm.; width, 27.5 cm.; height, 19 cm. Early eighteenth century. Yamato Bunkakan, Nara. (See also Figure 78.)

living, selling to keep from starving, resulted in the dark, somewhat warped side of Korin the artist. The facial expressions of his Vimalakirti and T'ai Kung-wang are used to substantiate this theory.

But this interpretation is unconvincing. Korin had a good bit of courage to his character; this plucky streak is seen in his letters, and nothing in his work shows him to have been cowed or embittered by his financial straits. This forces us to recognize in the dark side of Korin's work a conscious attitude grounded in the way in which he personally encountered his world. Repugnance, cynicism, and disdain were the mixture of feelings that formed his attitude toward Genroku life. He felt contempt for a world lulled into soft living by a long peace; disdain for the static, passive way of life of warrior, farmer, and merchant alike; and cynicism toward a world given over to frivolity and license.

Some may object to this interpretation, insisting that Korin was also a child of his times. Had not Genroku been good to him, too? Had he not taken advantage of its pleasures? He might have done well to turn more of his sneering inward.

The point is well taken: Korin had been second to none in his pursuit of worldly pleasures. But I would defend him if only for the polish of the pleasures he sought. He had a refinement of taste and a rich sense of enjoyment imbued by his upbringing in one of the great houses of the Kan'ei *machishu*. He had the inherent *savoir faire* of the elite and an inbred love for the classical nobility. Rich endowments such as these gave originality and creativity even to his pleasures.

Examples are the "picnic lunch" and "black and white costume" incidents. In the former, we watch him cleverly one-upping his companions with their

100. Ogata Korin: White Plum Blossoms. *Incense wrapper mounted on a hanging scroll. Colors on gold foil over silk; height, 17.9 cm.; width, 15 cm. Early eighteenth century.*

101. Ogata Korin: Morning Glories. *Incense wrapper mounted on a hanging scroll. Colors on gold foil over silk; height, 26.2 cm.; width, 21.1 cm. Early eighteenth century.*

gold-lacquered lunch boxes by unveiling his own tidbits wrapped in simple bamboo skin decorated inside with shimmering gold leaf, then casually discarding the wrappers in a nearby stream. In the other episode, at a fashion contest for the Kyoto upper class, we see him manipulating the award for the winning ensemble so as to go to a woman wearing only a simple white kimono with a black silk over-jacket—while her lady-in-waiting wore a stunning garment of gorgeous colors. Korin's amusements amounted to more than plebeian pursuit of crude pleasures. He had the artist's disdain for everything philistine; and it was this set of mind that informed all his art in one way or another. The last of a dying elite, he had an aristocratic loathing for the boorishness of the new bourgeoisie. This attitude is at the core of his work.

Protest had been a Hon'ami family tradition. As Koetsu and Sotatsu had sought to enclose them-selves entirely within the world of the classical, so too did Korin wall himself off into a world of his own. But more than with Koetsu or Sotatsu, Korin's retreat into classicism was a strong personal assertion. Thus, the monument he erected in the demanding field of decorative art rose out of himself; his convictions were expressed in one new idea after another, blazing a trail that seemed designed to thwart any would-be followers. The gift of social protest spurred him on. The dark side we note in some of his work was indeed of his essence as a man, a strange source of inspiration and creativity.

Korin died in 1716 at the age of fifty-eight. His two decades as an artist, including his years in Edo from 1704 until about 1710, were sustained throughout by a sense of personal protest and independence that gave his art an immortal quality transcending its Genroku origins. It was to Korin that the proud *machishu* culture owed its final glory.

CHAPTER SEVEN

The Life and Art of Kenzan

KENZAN'S YOUTH   Kenzan lived a stormy life of eighty years. But in contrast to Korin's life, where tempests raged for all to see, Kenzan's took place in quiet, far from the crowd. As a young man he received an inheritance from his father, then proceeded to change his name from Gombei to Shinsho (Deep Reflection) in keeping with his retirement to the secluded Shuseido, a Zen hermitage that he was building at the entrance to Ninna-ji temple. He was twenty-six years old at the time.

The hermitage was finished in the fall of 1690, and Kenzan invited his friend and fellow Zen disciple Gettan to write something for the occasion. The latter did so, leaving us the beautiful lines of the *Shuseido-ki* (Shuseido Record), treating of Kenzan's seclusion: "Where water is quiet, one can see even a single hair in its reflection; where the earth is quiet, anything may rest thereon. The man who does not quietly pursue the path of Zen has a troubled heart and confused mind; peace of spirit is unattainable. Dear Shinsho, please understand this and strive for silence. Earnest striving, for however long it takes, leads naturally to an understanding of life."

The life of the recluse, however, was not for Kenzan a way of forsaking the world. On the contrary, it offered the ultimate in refined pleasure, the reverse of Korin's profligate life. For Kenzan the Shuseido was a quiet retreat, away from the garish luxury of Genroku. Popular amusements and mundane life were unbearable to an esthete of his highly idealistic nature. He shared the taste for originality and refinement that Korin was seeking amid dissolute pleasures. He sought a creative kind of seclusion from a strong sense of protest against the times. But he wished for an untrammeled life of the spirit where his own interests alone would thread everything together; and Zen was one way to attain this.

Kenzan was already a person of no mean culture. He was conversant with Chinese poetry and literature, the *waka* classics, and Confucianism; he knew Noh and *chanoyu* well. He was most skilled in calligraphy and had a great devotion to Koetsu, visiting the Hon'ami residence in Takagamine to enjoy hearing recollections of Koetsu from his grandson Kuchusai Koho (1601–82). He devoted himself to calligraphy in emulation of Koetsu.

Kenzan's later calligraphy changed, showing more breadth; but in his younger period it was very correct, in the Chinese manner. In the *Ototsuka ni Yogiru no Ki* (Fig. 102), which he wrote in 1692 at the age of twenty-nine, we find eloquent verse and a script of refreshing beauty. He writes of the master of the Shisendo at Ototsuka, the poet Ishikawa Jozan: "My master's verse emulates the Chinese style and has the elegance of old. His virtue extends to the heavens above and foreign lands below. In the morning of the flower or the evening of the moon, he always speaks to men of learning, never failing to evoke interest; disdaining

過凹凸窠記

今蘇壬申首夏步自隻岡之艸堂
將遊洛東矣四明之南鴨川之東
到于一林蓁號一乘寺藪里而八
大天王穩坐地也石莖表之修松樹
森々古怪可觀居民歸曰下松矣行東

餅情不盡賦一絕詠主人
遶帯鴨流詩獨此翠圍凹凸
映高樓詩僊堂上無邊興
留我幾思紅葉秋

習静堂霊海省稧省書

102. Ogata Kenzan: Ototsuka ni Yogiru no Ki. 1692.

sullied riches, his purity rejoices in poverty: no wife or child in his life." These lines indicate how deeply moved Kenzan was by Jozan's life. He too remained unmarried, perhaps in emulation.

The Shuseido ideals were to be set aside earlier than expected, however. Inside ten years, Kenzan had gone through his inheritance money and, faced with the Kariganeya crisis, took up life together with Korin. Both resolved to push past the problems besetting them, Korin as a painter and Kenzan as a potter.

THE NARUTAKI KILN Kenzan's decision to undertake the vocation of ceramist was made at the gate of Ninna-ji temple in the presence of the famous potter Ninsei. He had long since studied pottery here as a pastime, and Koetsu's grandson Koho had taught him Raku ware methods at Takagamine. But it had been little more than an amateur's pleasant diversion enjoyed in solitude. He was to call up a skill far beyond that of an amateur in the years that lay ahead and would be ranked as one of Japan's three greatest potters. Now pottery had to become both hobby and source of income. Kenzan set his mind to it, and in 1699 received permission from Ninna-ji temple to build a kiln at Izumidani and undertake the potter's trade. In August he was initiated into the secrets of the craft by Ninsei; the kiln was completed in September and fired for the first time in November. This was the Narutaki kiln and the birth of what is called "Kenzan ware."

Korin lent a willing hand to his younger brother's work. In the beginning, as Kenzan recorded in the *Edo Densho*, his book of pottery recipes, after the initial firing Korin did the painting, after

103. Ogata Kenzan: "Diadem" oblong dish. Length, 19.2 cm.; width, 9.7 cm. Early eighteenth century. Fujita Art Museum, Osaka.

which Kenzan would inscribe or engrave the back. It was a joint project. Samples of this ware are still on hand (Figs. 3, 72, 79, 86, 87). Eventually Kenzan also took up the brush, adding his own design innovations to those of Korin. He labored long at glaze techniques and shaping, bit by bit improving his craftsmanship until he was turning out work he was not ashamed to sell. To judge by the frequency with which it is mentioned, Kenzan ware seems to have enjoyed a good reputation.

The Narutaki kiln operation, though an aid to learning ceramic techniques, never became a financial success. Kenzan's work inevitably bore the mark of a cultivated man's avocation; his kind of work was not suited to the high costs and risks of the business of commercial pottery production. There was also the fact of his unwillingness to sell anything that failed to meet his own standards.

Perfectionist, ever eager to learn, Kenzan worked at design painting in both the Chinese and Japanese styles; he apparently studied copies of imported Western ware, as well. Yet the kiln never amounted to a going concern, with profit taking second place to the pleasure of creation. The kiln was operated in this fashion for thirteen years, but finally in 1712 its fires flickered and died. The Narutaki years must be seen as a time of testing for Kenzan and his potter's skills, a time that gave him the confidence to declare that there was no soil on earth unfit for potter's clay.

There was a great output from the Narutaki kiln, but the pieces we can certify as authentic Kenzan are few. In addition to the plates he and Korin produced, there are the crosshatched incense container with plum blossoms (Fig. 108) and the "Waterfall" tea bowl (Figs. 80, 150), both fine examples. The

104. Ogata Kenzan: tea bowl
with painting of lotus and king-
fisher. Black Raku ware; diameter,
10.4 cm. Early eighteenth century.

105 (right). Ogata Kenzan:
"Thistle" tea bowl. Diameter,
9.7 cm. 1737.

106. Ogata Kenzan: view of Mount Horai. Illustration from the pottery recipes section of Sano Tebikaecho *(Sano Diaries). 1737.*

Chinese-style painting on these early pieces is intense and strong; the colors have the charm and appealing unaffectedness of Yamato-e, and the calligraphy is full of dignity and feeling. This is the famous Kenzan ware well in hand, an impressive overall blend of pottery, painting, and calligraphy. Through studying Koetsu's many exquisite combinations of script and painting or gold lacquer, Kenzan originated an entirely new form of ceramics.

THE CHOJIYAMACHI KILN

Kenzan was fifty years old when he moved from Narutaki to Nijo Chojiyamachi, faced with the serious problem of making ends meet. He was the disciple of Ninsei and had brought along from Narutaki his pupil Ihachi, who was Ninsei's son by birth but now Kenzan's by adoption. Maintaining a small kiln at Shogo-in temple, he turned out a constant flow of ceramics for sale, adapting his well-known Kenzan ware, which had a high reputation, to the popular taste. Large amounts were sold in the Gojosaka and Shimo-Awataguchi districts of Kyoto. Meanwhile, Korin had returned from Edo, apparently to take up where he had left off doing the painting on Kenzan's ware. A typical piece from this period is the square dish with the poet Huang Shan-ku watching sea gulls, seen in Figures 86 and 107.

These were rather grim days for Kenzan, without his previous consolations of seclusion or the chance to obey his muse freely. Moreover, how could he bring himself to eke out a living by selling products he felt to be inferior? He probably sought relief from such inner conflicts in painting, calligraphy, and further pursuit of his ceramic studies.

107. Ogata Kenzan: inscription on the back of square dish with painting of Huang Shan-ku watching sea gulls. Length, 22 cm.; width, 22.1 cm.; height, 3 cm. Early eighteenth century. Tokyo National Museum. (See also Figure 86.)

The Chojiyamachi period spanned twenty years. During this time Korin died. Kenzan was alone, without a family, turning out great quantities of Kenzan ware. Perhaps we have somewhat denigrated the artistic value of the work he did in Chojiyamachi. Research to dispel our doubts, however, is still nonexistent, leaving us for the moment bound to consider this period as Kenzan's "dark night of the soul."

As a young man his sole joy had been his friendship with Prince Nijo (Tsunahira, a fellow Zen student and esthete), upon whom he was often in attendance with Korin. A public record in Kyoto notes the frequent visits of parties including Korin and Kenzan between 1689 and 1720. As attendants to Tsunahira, the brothers were also his companions in recreation; they presented him with paintings and pottery and tutored him in the arts. Even after

Korin died, Kenzan continued in sole attendance, and the aging friends probably reminisced often of the good old days. Kenzan loved learning, was always an artist at heart, and must have found most congenial the salon atmosphere of Nijo, with its coterie of court nobles and upper-class Genroku merchants.

THE MOVE TO EDO   It is difficult to surmise why Kenzan should have decided to forsake Kyoto for Edo in 1731 at the age of sixty-eight. In the *Sano Tebikaecho* (Sano Diaries) he is described as "leaving the emperor's court in disgrace." No mention of the nature of the problem is made, but there must have been a serious reason why a man of so many years' sojourn in the capital could not remain and had to move to Edo. It is not difficult to guess Kenzan's emotions

108. *Ogata Kenzan: incense container with painting of plum blossoms and crosshatching. Height, 4.8 cm. Early eighteenth century. Fujita Art Museum, Osaka.*

109. *Ogata Kenzan: lily-shaped bowl. Rust painting; diameter, 16.1 cm. Early eighteenth century.*

as he set out for the other city with Prince Kokan, who had long favored Kenzan with his patronage.

In Edo Kenzan eventually built a kiln at Iriya Village and started making pottery again. He turned out traditional Kenzan ware and Raku ware. Although we are still unable to identify any particular piece as Iriya kiln work, Kenzan, a potter to the core, probably never let the sun go down without producing something. Yet for all this, he was very much an exile in Edo. He had been deeply hurt, and, sensitive person that he was, a masterpiece would have been quite beyond him at this juncture.

KENZAN'S WORK AT SANO

Life went on for five years in Edo, until one day in 1736 when, through the Fuyuki family, he received an invitation that was to change his life once again. The source of this and a number of previous invitations were Okawa Kendo and Sudo Tosen of Sano in what is now Tochigi Prefecture, north of Tokyo. They were influential landlords, controlling key irrigation points in Watarase and Otone, and were the "aristocracy" of the area. Having heard that Kenzan was in Edo, they invited him to come to Sano. At first, Kenzan was reluctant; Sano was deep in the country, even farther away from Kyoto than was Edo, and he was getting too old for travel. He declined for a while but eventually gave in, planning a brief visit of two or three months. In the spring of 1737 he boarded a boat and was escorted by Sudo Tosen to his destination. As it turned out, the visit lengthened into a stay of over a year. Even in his wildest dreams, Kenzan never could have expected to see the final fruit of his efforts here.

110. *Ogata Kenzan: two views of dish shaped like a Chinese bell flower and with a painting of plum blossoms. Diameter, 33.8 cm. 1737.*

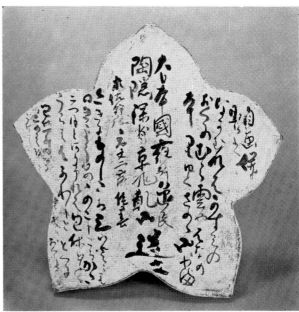

111. Ogata Kenzan: excerpt from
Sano Tebikaecho (Sano Diaries).
1737.

The hospitability was warm at Sano, and for all its remoteness the place was a bustle of boats bringing goods in and out, and many members of the cultural elite came to visit. Tosen and his circle were men of culture and learning, and they looked up to Kenzan as a master. It was like being back among friends. Cheered by his warm welcome, he set up a kiln and went about his craft, giving his products as presents to various people in Sano, sharing his technical knowledge and his joy in the making of pottery. He made short jaunts here and there, including a trip to Nikko, recording his impressions en route. In the end, his stay lasted well into the following year.

The work of Kenzan at Sano is called "Sano Kenzan," and it is proving most valuable for our study of his work. The freshness and technical flair of the work done here brought to perfection all the skills he had used up to this time. His more than

twenty years of effort at Chojiyamachi and Edo seemed to explode in a brilliant display of Kenzan's art at its best (Figs. 82, 83, 84, 105, 110, 112, 151, 152). With more than two hundred superb Sano pieces to choose from, we have just what we need to formulate a good estimation of his art.

The most perfect examples of Kenzan's creative blend of calligraphy, painting, and ceramics are found in endless variety among his Sano wares. Kenzan's calligraphy is versatile, easily following either the Chinese or Japanese style or freely combining them, giving us a synthesis of his insights in exquisite script. The pottery painting includes both *Kanga* and Yamato-e, drawing from both Sotatsu and Korin and finally jelling in the distinctive form known as the Kenzan style. His brilliant coloring is the outcome of long years of effort; minus the sentimental quality of Ninsei, his master, it is rich and virile. The painting and calligraphy

112. Ogata Kenzan: front (far left) and back of decorative tile with a painting of a plum tree and crescent moon. Length, 26.5 cm.; width, 26.1 cm. 1737.

are executed gracefully, always deferring to the shape of the piece. The cumulative effect of the whole—script, painting, and pottery—is a feast for the eye. It is creativity that is free as a breeze. Kenzan is never more beautiful than here.

Upon returning from Sano, Kenzan planned to work his Iriya kiln again. It had survived the great fire of 1737, but his house had not; so he had to move into one of a row of boarding houses on the right bank of the Sumida River in Fukagawa, where the river enters Tokyo Bay. This made the kiln inconvenient, and as a result his work did not go well. He did more painting than pottery, and we have many such works done between his seventy-sixth and eighty-first years. The vigor and verve of the Sano period, however, are missing.

DEATH CAME to Kenzan in the year 1743. It is recorded that he left no heir and had no one to settle affairs after his demise. Jirobei, his landlord, took care of the funeral arrangements, and Prince Ueno is recorded as having donated one *ryo* (an old unit of coinage) to cover expenses.

From his younger days of seclusion when he retreated from society at Shuseido until he died on a tenement sickbed, Kenzan's solitary life was one long love affair with beauty. It was a quest for the pure and genuine. His heart was full of love for humanity and nature; his keen and unaffected poetic perception never clouded.

Among Japanese artists—perhaps even among all artists—I can think of no one who cared for flowers more. Japanese people traditionally love nature and cherish flowers as one of life's joys, and Kenzan's art expresses this most basic feeling. He must have painted thousands of flowers over his long career. He immersed himself in their bouquet, painting them and firing them into pottery, where

113. Ogata Kenzan: snow section of the Sano Tebikaecho *(Sano Diaries). 1737.*

they bloomed as never before. Flowers enhanced the beauty of Kenzan's art; but Kenzan's art also enhanced the beauty of flowers.

This is why, even though Kenzan took issue with his times, he never became negative or despairing of the world. His heart was completely open to the beauty of nature, devoid of Korin's abrasive cynicism. His sincerity touches the heart. When we are puzzled over the nature of beauty, there is Kenzan, showing us his flowers, as if to say: "Look at the flowers. Their beauty does not lie."

Nevertheless, we sense a strain of sadness in Kenzan's works and wonder why. Is it a sadness directed at those who cannot understand the beauty of flowers and so are deceived by a false beauty? I cannot believe his was a sadness at his solitude, at living and dying alone. No artist was ever so blessed in a give-and-take of love with his friends

the flowers. His relationship with nature was so close as to surpass even Sotatsu's. His sadness was, I think, that of the poet. He was so immersed in nature that the very intensity of his love would leave him with an empty feeling. Is this not the sadness of existence itself?

Not Genroku, not the vision of a fading elite or of freedom in art, was that important to Kenzan. Even beauty seemed sometimes to fade. It was life, so fragile and fleeting, that he experienced. He expressed something of this feeling at Sano in his lotus dish (Fig. 84). It has a pink and a white flower against a darker ground, and in the upper right-hand corner is an inscription that reads: *Jakumetsu joshin.* This is a Buddhist term describing the attainment of that pure state of total awareness known as nirvana—and it describes the mind of Kenzan in much of his life and work.

CHAPTER EIGHT

The Successors of Sotatsu and Korin

THE FOUR MASTERS   We have considered the works of the four artists Koetsu, Sotatsu, Korin, and Kenzan in order to see how each encountered his own world. I think that it is now evident that all were in some way at odds with their times. Their work also had in common the decorative-art genre and that beautiful dialogue with nature that is so profoundly Japanese. But the shared antipathy toward the times implicit in their works is their most striking common characteristic.

Traditionally, decorative art has been conformist, its very existence dependent on producing whatever society might demand. The voicing of protest or of the artist's personal opinion has usually been thought of as a hindrance in the field of decorative art; but here were four men who expressed strong protest, yet yielded to none as decorative artists and even assumed the first rank in their generations. In this lies their greatness.

Artists are always stimulated in their work by a certain clash with their surroundings. But should they feel utterly helpless before a situation or, as sometimes happens, so full of themselves that self-righteousness vitiates the message, their statement loses its power to persuade; it becomes a display of hasty, immature resistance and does not achieve a universal beauty.

But this was not the case with our four artists.

They were gifted in the ability to express their intentions completely. Because of the universality of the beauty they created, the resistance they felt in their hearts did not arouse resistance in others. The result was that the establishment that they fought so fiercely welcomed them like brilliant though illegitimate children.

Their common choice of nature, especially flowers, as subjects was a master stroke. Nothing on earth reaches the hearts of all as do flowers; they move everyone without distinction. A flower is beauty incarnate, the purest example of what beauty is all about. Japanese art has not been sidetracked on esthetic backroads perhaps because it has always been haunted in one way or another by the beauty of flowers. By continuing this native artistic heritage, Koetsu, Sotatsu, Korin, and Kenzan gave their art a universal beauty. As for the thrust of their protest, it was kept from surfacing but was redirected so as to yield a beauty all the more compelling.

But we should also ask: Who surrounded these four masters of decorative art? Who came after them, and what kind of artists were they? What kind of art did they produce? These questions deserve answers; and it may be that the only reason for the obscurity of those who came after is the superlative art of the four great masters.

114. Sosetsu: detail of Autumn Grasses. *Pair of sixfold screens. Colors on gold foil over paper; dimensions of each screen: height, 184 cm.; width, 464 cm. C. mid-seventeenth century.*

Koetsu and Sotatsu were surrounded by many artisans and assistants. In one sense these men were unfortunate. Aside from Kamiya Soji and Fudeya Myoki, they remain anonymous. Yet without their work Koetsu could never have produced his pottery and gold-lacquer masterpieces; nor could Sotatsu have realized his gold-and-silver paintings, his fans and screens. For decorative art by definition requires the work of many craftsmen. These valuable helpers are nameless, but we should not for that reason forget them.

KOSA AND KOHO Kosa (1578–1637), who was the adopted son of Koetsu, was known as a master in the Hon'ami family business. His painting, like the man himself, was of a warm, gentle nature. Almost nothing has

come down to us except his *Cypress* fan painting (Fig. 117), but this reveals much of his character.

Kosa's son Koho (1601–82) went by the name of Kuchusai. He sculpted a wooden bust of Koetsu (Fig. 23), made Raku ware in his grandfather's fashion, and is known for his "Winter Moon" tea bowl. He is said to have been a worthy successor to preside over Takagamine.

SOSETSU We have already mentioned Sotatsu's disciple Sosetsu. His most famous works are the *Autumn Grasses* screens (Fig. 114), which are an Important Cultural Property, and the cedar doors, painted in 1639, in the Yoju-ji temple in Sakai. Many works bearing Sotatsu's name are thought to be actually the work of Sosetsu. The use he made of Sotatsu's seal, the Inen,

115. *Fukae Roshu: detail of* Ivy Walk. *Pair of sixfold screens. Colors on gold foil over paper; dimensions of each screen: height, 146.3 cm.; width, 247.7 cm. C. mid-eighteenth century.*

was not as a student deferring to his master but rather for purposes of business identification, for he was Sotatsu's successor at the Tawaraya. Although his work is not of the quality of Sotatsu's, Sosetsu nevertheless carved out his own niche and had evident technique; and through him "Tawaraya painting" became popular with a wider public. He differed from Sotatsu and Koetsu in not being at variance with his times. Like the *machishu* forced to bow to feudal rule, his conformity to the demands of the day is very noticeable.

SHIKO, KAGEI,
AND ROSHU

Around the time of Korin and Kenzan there also lived Watanabe Shiko, Fukae Roshu, and Tatebayashi Kagei. Shiko, who lived from 1683 to 1755, went over to Korin from the Kano school.

His Kano-style autumn landscape screens and Korin-style *Flowers and Grasses of the Four Seasons* screens (Fig. 116) are representative and exude a real warmth of feeling. He worked with Kenzan when the latter was at Narutaki, helping in the painting. His dishes with paintings of poems for the twelve months and other works have come down to us.

Fukae Roshu was the son of Fukae Shozaemon, like Korin's patron Nakamura Kuranosuke an official of the mint. He was born in 1699 and died in 1757. His style was similar to that of Sotatsu, and he has left us many flower paintings, together with *Ivy Walk* paintings (Fig. 115) based on Sotatsu's *Ivy Walk shikishi*, which dealt with themes from the *Ise Monogatari*.

Tatebayashi Kagei, also called Shirai Soken, was

116. *Watanabe Shiko: detail of* Flowers and Grasses of the Four Seasons. *Pair of sixfold screens. Colors on paper; dimensions of each screen: height, 124.2 cm.; width, 265.7 cm. Eighteenth century.*

active around 1736–40. He became a student of Kenzan when the latter was in Edo. His *Crossing to Sano* screens show the influence of Sotatsu through Kenzan, and a brilliant sense of color.

SAKAI HOITSU   The most famous name in Rimpa—the Korin style of painting—is Sakai Hoitsu. He was born in 1761 and died in 1828. The second son of Sakai Tadatsugu, lord of Himeji Castle, he was an ardent disciple of Korin as well as a *haiku* poet and man of letters. He was also a playboy of the caliber of Korin. Hoitsu did many paintings, adding a certain flair to Korin's splendid painting style. His *Flowers in a Rainstorm* screens and *Musashino* screens (Fig. 120) are his most representative works. Three books published by Hoitsu provide important materials for Rimpa research: *Korin Hyakuzu* (One Hundred Paintings by Korin) and *Ogata-ryu Inpu* (Seals of the Ogata School), both of which appeared in 1815; and *Kenzan Iboku* (Kenzan's Ink Paintings). These have been of great value for Rimpa studies, but Hoitsu cannot be credited with giving us the real Korin, as he rendered Korin largely in terms of his own taste.

Shiko and Kagei, Roshu and Hoitsu fall far short of the stature of Korin and Kenzan both in talent and in life-style. Hoitsu was the most gifted, but his art ultimately took on the color of his overripe, decadent age, with a culture in decline and a people lulled into somnolence by peace. Hoitsu seemingly lacked the fiber to do other than drift with the tide, and this shows in his art; his is nice painting, no more.

117. Hon'ami Kosa: Cypress. *Fan painting mounted on a hanging scroll. Colors on paper; height, 13.4 cm.; width, 35 cm. Itsuo Art Museum, Osaka.*

118. Nakamura Hochu: Mount Fuji. *Fan painting mounted on a hanging scroll. Ink and light colors on paper; height, 20.2 cm.; width, 52.5 cm. Early nineteenth century.*

119. Morimura Hogi: Red Plum Blossoms. *Fan painting mounted on a hanging scroll. Ink and colors on paper; height, 16.5 cm.; width, 45 cm. C. mid-nineteenth century.*

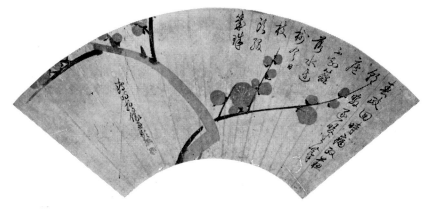

120. *Sakai Hoitsu: detail of* Musashino. *Pair of sixfold screens. Colors on gold foil over paper; dimensions of each screen: height, 139.5 cm.; width, 307.2 cm. Late eighteenth century.*

HOCHU AND KIITSU I would recommend as more worthy of praise the work of Nakamura Hochu, a contemporary of Hoitsu who lived in Osaka. His painting techniques have the Rimpa trademarks to perfection: *tarashi-komi,* the dropping of a darker ink or color onto the still-wet surface of a prior painting, and *tamekomi,* its reverse—the absorption of color or ink back into the brush from the painting surface. He opened new horizons with his original figure, landscape, and—most notably—flower paintings. His facile, forthright brush suited all these subjects and techniques, surely putting him in the first rank (Fig. 118).

Hochu's student Suzuki Kiitsu, who was in the service of the prominent Sakai family, was an artist of superb technique, though his works are few. Some are in Hoitsu's style, but Kiitsu deserves praise for going beyond this to a personal expression of his own. His *Plum and Camellia* screens (Fig. 121) and *Snake Gourd* fan painting are bold compositions with generous brushwork; they brought a breath of fresh air into the mannerism into which Korin-style painting had fallen in the early decades of the nineteenth century.

Rimpa had many advocates to carry it through the Edo period. Among *bunjin* (literati) themes painted in Rimpa style we occasionally find works of interest. An example is the fine painting of Morimura Hogi (1807–62), who effected a harmonization of Chinese poetry and the Korin style in the manner of Kenzan (Fig. 119). Also active at this time were the *nanga* (Chinese Southern-school painting) artists, led by Ike no Taiga, who made this genre more Japanese in feeling.

121. *Suzuki Kiitsu: detail of* Plum and Camellia. *Pair of sixfold screens. Colors on paper; dimensions of each screen: height, 144.5 cm.; width, 309 cm. Early nineteenth century.*

THE MODERN PERIOD The curtain finally rang down on the Edo period in 1868 with the Meiji Restoration and the end of Japan's isolation. Like a tide long stemmed, Western culture rushed in, naturally bringing about a tremendous upheaval in the Japanese art world. Japanese artists, faced with the Western painting tradition, began seriously questioning the direction Japanese painting should take. The Nippon Bijutsu-in (Japan Academy of Art), founded in 1893, was a kind of laboratory for testing new directions. Okakura Tenshin and Ernest Fenollosa founded it, and Okakura was central in leading a serious attempt to recover Japan's artistic past. Studies were conducted on the handling of Western painting techniques. Sotatsu and Korin were rediscovered, and their techniques were reinterpreted.

Yokoyama Taikan (1868–1958), Hishida Shunso (1847–1911), and other ultra-impressionists borrowed the Western technique of using no outline. The influence of Sotatsu's and Korin's non-outlining techniques can also be noted. Imamura Shiko (1880–1916) looked back nostalgically to the world of Sotatsu and revived it with new feeling (Fig. 122). Sotatsu and Korin soared in popularity as historical studies progressed. The growing interest in genuinely Japanese art influenced nearly every artist in one way or another. The artists of the Meiji (1868–1912), Taisho (1912–26), and Showa (1926–) eras, led by such prominent painters as Hayami Gyoshu (1926–), Maeda Seison (1885–), Kobayashi Kokei (1883–1957), and Yamaguchi Hoshun (1893–), were all indebted to Sotatsu and Korin to some degree.

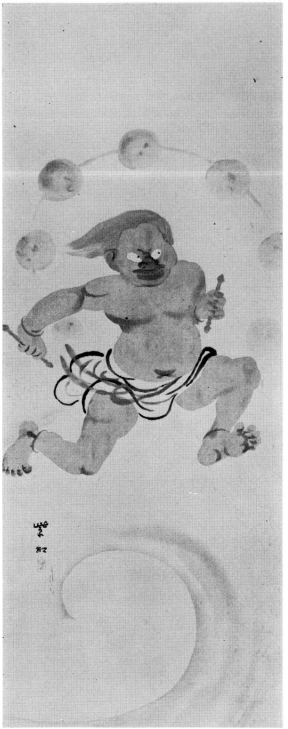

122. Imamura Shiko: detail of God of
Wind and God of Thunder. *Pair of
hanging scrolls. Colors on silk; dimensions of
each scroll: height, 108 cm.; width, 41.2
cm. 1911. Tokyo National Museum.*

123. Gyoshu: detail of Camellia Tree. *Pair of twofold screens. Colors on gold foil over paper; dimensions of each screen: height, 167 cm.; width, 169 cm. 1929.*

The tradition of Kenzan was perpetuated by Miura Ken'ya (1825–89), Ogata Kensai (a sixth-generation descendant of Kenzan), and others. This style has remained a living tradition right up to the present through the pottery of the late Tomimoto Kenkichi and of Bernard Leach.

Today, decorative art is in. "Art for art's sake" and individual expression are out. In every field we see art, like the crafts, coming more and more into demand as a vehicle to enrich our daily lives. This was the situation at the time of Sotatsu and Korin. I see in this a new development in contemporary art. And in precisely such times as these do Sotatsu and Korin and their immense artistic achievements have much to say to us. Study of their significance in the context of art history is important; but more important, I would suggest, is reviving their work in our own lives by trying, like them, to make life more beautiful. Is this not the challenge of the contemporary artist?

CHAPTER NINE

The Works of Koetsu

CERAMICS   We can divide the works of Koetsu into two categories: those which he himself produced and those which he only designed. His pottery and calligraphy belong to the first category; his gold-lacquer, painting, and printing work fall into the second. Consequently, Koetsu's individuality as an artist shines forth most in his ceramics and calligraphy, while his artistic ideals emerge most clearly in his gold lacquer, gold-and-silver paintings, and Saga books.

KOETSU POLISHED his pottery technique with the help of Raku Jokei and his son Donyu. This father-and-son team improved upon the Raku ware of the Kyoto potter Tanaka Chojiro (1516–92), originator of the type. They fired pottery at higher temperatures and devised a special glaze. This resulted in tea bowls of a beautiful luster. Koetsu's work was to be Raku ware of this kind. Since these new techniques were developed by the Raku father-and-son team sometime during the first decade of the seventeenth century, Koetsu must have begun making pottery thereafter. This would mean that he embarked on a study of the Raku family's clay and glazing techniques when he was in his mid-fifties. Then, moving to Takagamine, he built his own kiln and began making the tea bowls we now know.

One feature of Koetsu's tea bowls is the painstaking care and skill shown in shaping each and every piece. The shapes of Raku ware faithfully reflect the maker. The mild-mannered craftsman fashions a gentle shape; the forceful person produces a forceful one. The shape of Koetsu's bowls show him to have been a man of great character and vigor.

Koetsu's representative pieces—"Oto Goze" and "Bishamondo" (Figs. 21, 22), "Mount Fuji" (Fig. 24) and "Autumn Shower" (Fig. 126)— all have different shapes, yet they share a common richness and vigor. Each has its own individuality; no two are alike in form, use of the spatula, or molding of the foot. Each shows us another facet of Koetsu's greatness. Moreover, behind their vigor Koetsu's bowls have a polish and sophistication befitting upper-class *machishu* art.

The dignity of the famous "Mount Fuji" tea bowl, the grace of "Autumn Shower," the richness of "Rain Clouds," the pervasive strength of "Bishamondo," the bright splendor of "Oto Goze"— these qualities blend to form a rich portrait of Koetsu, a strong, attractive personality rising out of the Kyoto cultural tradition. Just as we find ourselves gazing raptly at these works today, seized by their beauty, so too, I think, did discriminating people of the court and *machishu* of old.

LACQUERWARE   The "Boat-bridge" gold-lacquer writing box (Fig. 26) bespeaks both Koetsu's affection for the classical past and his aptitude for design. His eye for design is evident in the lid of the box, which swells like the gentle slope of Takagamine. In raised lacquer on a

124. *Hon'ami Koetsu and Tawaraya So-tatsu: detail of* Thousand Cranes. *Hand scroll with painting by Sotatsu and calligraphy by Koetsu. Gold-and-silver underpainting on paper; height, 34.1 cm.; length, 1,460 cm. Early seventeenth century. (See also Figure 68.)*

125. *Tawaraya Sotatsu and Suminokura Soan: detail of* Ryutatsu-bushi *with painting of bamboo by Sotatsu and calligraphy by Soan. Block-printed gold-and-silver underpainting on paper; height, 33.5 cm. 1605.*

gold background is a boat, and over it a bridge formed by a band of lead. A poem in mother-of-pearl reads:

"The Road to Azuma at Sano Bridge.
Crossing, my heart crosses over to her.
Ah, my crossing that no one knows."

The billowed cover represents the arching of the bridge. The bold design of this work transforms Koetsu's longing for the past, as romanticized by the poem, into something marvelously suited to his own day. The box depicting a woodcutter (Fig. 20) also shows the shining beauty of Koetsu's lacquer art at its best.

CALLIGRAPHY　Koetsu's calligraphy is similarly rich. Let us examine it in the *waka* verses of scrolls shown in this book: *Thousand Cranes* (Figs. 68, 124) and *Flowers and Grasses of the Four Seasons* (Figs. 1, 8, 128). The broad, flowing hand seems never to lose its vigor and clarity despite the inherent difficulties of a writing surface made uneven by underpainting in gold and silver; it remains strong no matter how thin and delicate the stroke. His correspondence excepted, Koetsu's script is devoid of any fragility concomitant with increasing age. He grew older, but his script stayed young, retaining the vigorous stylistic ideal of the polished *waka* of the *Kokinshu* and *Shin Kokinshu* Heian-period anthologies.

Variations in Koetsu's calligraphic style according to period have yet to be discerned. And judging by the *shikishi* with gold-and-silver underpainting dated 1606, we can infer that there was not much change with time in either his *waka* scrolls or *shikishi*. I think that this is because the style he used, like that in the Saga books, he considered a

126 (above and left). Hon'ami Koetsu: two views of "Autumn Shower" tea bowl. Black Raku ware; diameter, 12.5 cm. Early seventeenth century.

127. Hon'ami Koetsu: "Rain Clouds" tea bowl. Black Raku ware; diameter, 12.4 cm. Early seventeenth century.

128. *Hon'ami Koetsu and Tawaraya Sotatsu: detail of* Flowers and Grasses of the Four Seasons. *Hand scroll with painting by Sotatsu and calligraphy by Koetsu. Gold-and-silver underpainting on paper; height, 34 cm. Early seventeenth century.*

particular form to be consciously striven for and adhered to at all times. Script must be seen as design for Koetsu, in this case a design devised specifically for the purpose of clothing ancient verse in modern garb.

The man himself, however, is mirrored most clearly in the script of his letters (Fig. 4). These offer a clear view of the greatness and strength of Koetsu as prominent upper-class *machishu*, Nichiren Buddhist, and head of the Hon'ami family.

WORKS THAT Koetsu and Sotatsu created together are not limited to those in which Koetsu executed the calligraphy and Sotatsu the painting. Koetsu turned his hand to design and painting, too.

Gold-and-silver painting went back as far as the Heian period. This tradition, together with that of a rather debilitated Yamato-e painting, had somehow managed to survive, and in the late Muromachi period and on through the Momoyama, the use of gold-and-silver painting was revived. But under Koetsu and Sotatsu it became more a transformation than a revival. They conceived of gold and silver less as paints than as brilliant components of the surface itself. For maximum effect these hues were used to cover the surface completely, the so-

called *betanuri* method. The need felt was for something in painting resembling the *surihaku* method in textiles, in which gold and silver patterns were printed on fabrics. It was the quest for such an effect in painting that resulted in the magnificent breakthroughs of Koetsu and Sotatsu in their gold-and-silver painting.

We can suppose that Sotatsu's painting was moving in this direction before he met Koetsu, but it was Koetsu who made a point of developing the method in his quest for an exquisite dialogue between underpainting and writing. Koetsu drafted designs, advised Sotatsu, and sometimes even painted. Once we begin to get a clear picture of the kind of person Koetsu was—his artistic aims and the decorative quality of his script, tea bowls, and lacquerware—we can discern his work in more than one gold-and-silver painting attributed to Sotatsu.

Sotatsu's cover and frontispiece for the *Heike Nokyo* scroll (Fig. 136), dated 1602, are thought to be his earliest gold-and-silver paintings. Then comes his block-printed gold-and-silver underpainting for the ballad known as *Ryutatsu-bushi*, dated 1605 (Fig. 125). The script is attributed to Suminokura Soan. There are also the *waka* scrolls with calligraphy by Koetsu and painting by So-

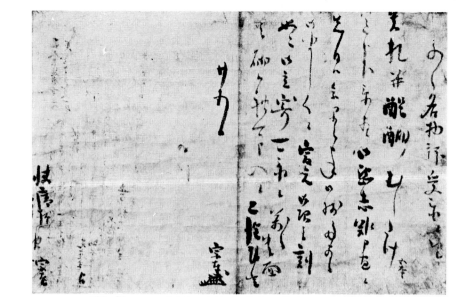

130. *Tawaraya Sotatsu: letter to Kaian. Early seventeenth century.*

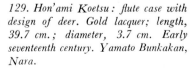

129. *Hon'ami Koetsu: flute case with design of deer. Gold lacquer; length, 39.7 cm.; diameter, 3.7 cm. Early seventeenth century. Yamato Bunkakan, Nara.*

tatsu; and in 1606 came Sotatsu's gold-and-silver-painted *shikishi*, again with Koetsu's script.

In 1607 appeared the text of a Noh songbook with Koetsu's writing and Sotatsu's underpainting block-printed in mica. This was followed by the *Hamamatsu* and *Wisteria* gold-and-silver fan paintings (Fig. 32). Around 1608 the Saga books (Fig. 5) were printed, a collaborative effort involving the calligraphy of Koetsu and Soan and the painting of Sotatsu. These were luxurious productions. The underpainting was block-printed in mica on paper, and over it was the beautiful script of one or the other calligrapher. These books, which include classics like the *Hojoki* and the later *Tsurezuregusa*, as well as Noh songbooks, exemplify the cultural spectrum of the Kyoto *machishu* elite. The early fruits of a joint effort, they were the forerunners of the great works that so beautifully combine Sotatsu's painting and Koetsu's script.

令聞給猶多忿嫉何

雖恐調撩調養法花

四衆八部人非人等也

大菩薩阿羅漢也人天

世能化主佛也弟子文

可甚見也其故在

如來在世猶多忿嫉難

生此土信此經人自

夫以末法流布時受

如說修行抄

131. Hon'ami Koetsu: detail of Nyosetsu Shugyosho *(Compendium of Discipline). Height, 39.1 cm. 1619. Hompo-ji, Kyoto.*

The recently discovered *Thousand Cranes waka* scroll seen in Figures 68 and 124 was among the first of these masterpieces. The flock of cranes, unifying the entire scroll with its magnificent rhythm, shows to perfection Sotatsu's rich talent under the guidance of Koetsu's sense of movement. The birds take off in perfect flight under Sotatsu's free-flowing brush, their graceful movement matched by the fluency and flourish of Koetsu's writing.

The *Flowers and Grasses of the Four Seasons* scrolls (Figs. 1, 8, 128) and the *Lotus* scroll (Fig. 40) exhibit the lavish gold-and-silver painting method at its peak. The gold and silver paints are developed to perfection as a medium, and Koetsu's elegant writing ranges easily over the brilliant surface. This is the culmination of *machishu* esthetics.

Not to be forgotten are the important contributions of Kamiya Soji, who labored so hard to produce the ideal paper for the task, and Fudeya Myoki the brush maker, as well as other artisans.

Parts of the *Deer* (Fig. 17) and *Lotus* scrolls contain a bold but somewhat amateurish brushwork unlike that of Sotatsu. The line is similar to that of Koetsu's script, and recognition of this has led to the attribution of these portions—correctly, in my estimation—to Koetsu.

CHAPTER TEN

The Works of Sotatsu

FAN PAINTINGS   It is only natural to begin discussing the many works of Sotatsu with his fan paintings. This I consider the best approach, because I consider his beginnings as a professional fan painter quite indisputable, and I believe that his superb sense of composition grew out of the approach he used in handling a fan-shaped surface for painting.

Among his fan paintings are the *Hamamatsu* and *Wisteria* pieces mentioned in the previous chapter, which date to 1607. In addition, there are the so-called *harimaze* screens—screens with a gold ground on which fan-paintings are then mounted. Famous examples are found in the Sambo-in at Daigo-ji temple in Kyoto (Figs. 11, 29, 133), in the Imperial Household Collection (Figs. 2, 13, 134, 138), and in private collections. Sotatsu-style painting is predominant, and we begin to realize how prolific his Tawaraya was.

Recently the opinion has gained ground that Tawaraya work covered a broad spectrum, the atelier turning out *shikishi, waka* scroll paper, fan paintings, paintings to be affixed to screens, and the like. It is not clear when all this began, but a reliable source reveals that Sotatsu had named his shop the Tawaraya before 1614. He probably founded it sometime around 1596, the teamwork with Koetsu commencing around 1605. Tawaraya fan paintings became famous in the second decade of the seventeenth century, so we can assume that the shop had been turning out work for some time by then.

In *Chikusai*, the description of famous places cited earlier and datable to some time between 1624 and 1644, "Tawaraya painting" is mentioned as famous for its *monogatari* illustrations. But it is probable that most of the Tawaraya's early fan paintings were flowers-and-grasses themes.

Fan painting began in Heian times with copies of sutras on fans and continued as an unbroken tradition down to the Genroku era, when it was one of the major genres of the town painters. It was popular in the capital in the late Muromachi period, too, just before Sotatsu's time, thanks to the Kyoto town painters of that day. Among recently discovered screen-mounted fan paintings are some in precisely this pre-Sotatsu town-painter style. Nearly all have flowers-and-grasses motifs or variations thereof. Such works are significant in light of the early Tawaraya fan paintings. Eventually, under Sotatsu, the classical world of *monogatari* painting would become popular in Kyoto. In this Sotatsu would draw heavily upon the classic learning of Koetsu and the upper-class *machishu*.

The distinctive feature of town-painter fan work is its striking composition. This was a natural outcome of the voluminous output of fan-painting studios. As with the Kano and Tosa schools, the aim was not the production of unique works of art. These painters wished to turn out as many works as possible of a given design. They hit upon the kind of composition best suited to the fan-painting genre, then repeated it again and again. Here it may be

132. Letter by Ichijo Kaneto. 1630.

mentioned in passing that it is only the artist who slips into mannerism by repetition; the craftsman, on the other hand, becomes a master through repetition, and the quality of his work improves in proportion: this is a craftsman's axiom. And fan painting is basically a craft.

Sotatsu counted such craftsmanship among his skills. He would go on to receive recognition as a *hokkyo* and rank among the elite. But long before he met Koetsu, and though master of the Tarawaya, he was a craftsman at heart. He worked along with several others, decorating fans and doing gold-and-silver painting. His leaning was toward design, and his talent for composition developed naturally through use into the great technique we see in his *monogatari* paintings on fans.

Three works that are thought to be definitely attributable to Sotatsu have been chosen for color plates. They were selected from his fan paintings in

Daigo-ji, the Imperial Household Collection, and Myoho-in. *Farmhouses in Spring* (Fig. 11) in particular reveals Sotatsu's compositonal skill. It is a masterpiece of its kind. The composition radiates from the fan pivot, building on the arc of the fan. Without this kind of composition, the painting would not hang together. I would ask the reader to look closely at Figure 11 to see how artfully the three houses in the painting follow this compositional principle. Their shapes and colors, and even the rippling stream, reveal Sotatsu's firm sense of composition as well as express his personality. This type of composition markedly influenced Sotatsu's later screen art.

The screen-mounted fan paintings in Figure 13 show Sotatsu's superb handling of *monogatari* themes. They deal with one episode, the Battle of Rokugahara, from the *Heiji Monogatari*. Using gold and silver foil as well as paint, Sotatsu has

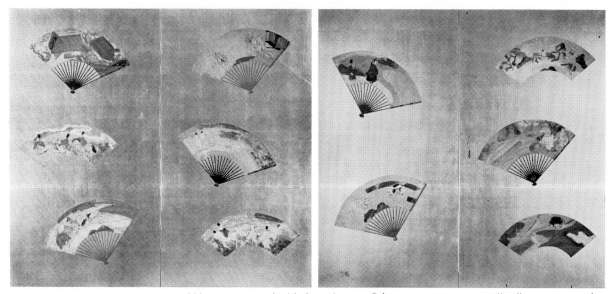

133. Tawaraya Sotatsu: Pair of twofold screens mounted with fan paintings. Colors on paper over gold foil; dimensions of each screen: height, 156 cm.; width, 168 cm. Early seventeenth century. Sambo-in, Daigo-ji, Kyoto. (See also Figures 11, 29.)

with his inimitable line and brilliant color created a magnificent work of art. This work sets the standard for Sotatsu's screen-mounted fans in the Imperial Household Collection.

The *Maples* fan of Figure 12, with its sharp contrast of scarlet on gold and its vivid and decorative pattern of leaves, is a good example of Sotatsu's floral-theme fan work.

A close analysis of the work of other fan paintings indicates that there were at least five more artists who probably belonged to the Tawaraya. Several of these paintings bear the Inen seal. Included are a number of fans that were made to be affixed to screens.

SCREENS AND PANELS   Next we consider Sotatsu's large surfaces. Among his flowers-and-grasses paintings in colors on a gold ground are the recently discovered *Musashino* (Fig. 37) and *Autumn Grasses* screens. These, together with the *Pine and Maple* and *Poppies* screens, the *Cherry Blossoms* sliding doors, and the *Flowers and Grasses* sliding doors bearing the Inen

seal (Fig. 9), have been attributed to Sotatsu, and we now have relatively rich sources for studying his large-surface paintings.

Since flowers and grasses comprised the original motifs of Tawaraya fan and gold-and-silver painting, it would be natural for Sotatsu to have carried such themes over into his screen and sliding-door painting. There are no grounds for the earlier theory that he did not himself paint flowers and grasses. We have sufficient proof that he did through the discovery of a letter (Fig. 132) from Ichijo Kaneto, a courtier, to Emperor Gomizuno-o, which reads: "By appointment to the Imperial Library: of the three pairs of screens requested, the plum tree set has the underpainting on gold foil completed. Thus says Sotatsu. More to follow."

The letter was written in 1630, which means that Sotatsu had been commissioned to do a plum screen, that is, a floral painting, thus proving beyond any shadow of a doubt that he did do work in this genre. It also tells us that Sotatsu was well known to the emperor and to Ichijo Kaneto and other people of rank, and that he was commis-

134. *Tawaraya Sotatsu: detail of a pair of eightfold screens mounted with fan paintings. Colors on paper over gold foil; dimensions of each screen; height, 111.5 cm.; width, 376 cm. Early seventeenth century. Imperial Household Collection.*

sioned to do paintings for them. As is proved here, Sotatsu was part of the court and *machishu* circle, and his works were of established repute.

The sliding-door painting reproduced in color in Figure 9 is executed in vibrant hues and superb brushwork over a gold ground. It far surpasses the *Cherry Blossoms* doors and the *Poppies* and *Pine and Maple* screens in technique and freshness of feeling, and ranks in quality with the *Musashino* screens. Comparing the doors with the floral motifs in Sotatsu's gold-and-silver paintings and *Life of Priest Saigyo* scroll has led me to the conclusion that because of their similarity of technique and feeling these doors, as well as the *Musashino* screens, belong to Sotatsu's early period. They are difficult to date exactly, but I would place them somewhere in the first decade of the seventeenth century, at about the time that Koetsu became aware of Sotatsu's gold-and-silver painting.

Acknowledged by Koetsu and reaffirmed in his vocation, Sotatsu eventually found himself commissioned to execute screens for the emperor in 1630. Thus he obviously continued to paint floral

themes. His style in this genre, as in his gold-and-silver painting, gained in richness and reached its peak under Koetsu's influence. The youthful keenness of his technique as seen in the sliding doors and *Musashino* screens, on the other hand, befits the skilled master of the Tawaraya in his years of growth as an artist.

Another characteristic feature of Sotatsu's *Flowers and Grasses* is the mode of composition. The painting is designed in such a way that its composition describes arcs leading to a point of greatest apparent depth at the center. This method, noticeable also in his later *Bugaku* screens, is an example of his "fan-surface" approach to composition and is another reason for considering the doors to be Sotatsu's work. In the *Musashino* screens, on the other hand, the composition unrolls in a scroll-like progression, as it does in his gold-and-silver *waka* scrolls. The fan-surface approach and the progressional approach together form Sotatsu's distinctive compositional methods.

The *Autumn Grasses*, *Pine and Maple*, and *Poppies* screens and the *Cherry Blossoms* sliding doors must be

attributed to another Tawaraya artist for reasons of composition and technique. Sosetsu comes immediately to mind. It was he who made the Sotatsu style in floral themes more decorative; he tended to stylization and, as pointed out earlier, was the precursor of Korin in methodology.

MONOGATARI THEMES   The *Genji Monogatari* screens are Sotatsu's greatest masterpieces in the *monogatari* genre. Among these are the "Sekiya" and "Miotsukushi" scenes (Fig. 10), now in the Seikado, Tokyo. We also have another "Sekiya" scene (Fig. 137) and other *Genji* screens. The *Heiji Monogatari* fans (Fig. 13), the *Ise Monogatari shikishi* paintings (Figs. 19, 139), and the *Life of Priest Saigyo* scrolls (Figs. 15, 16, 42) also comprised part of Sotatsu's classical world. He was familiarized with these themes through association with Koetsu and his circle of court and *machishu* elite. He also learned a great deal by studying old scrolls directly, and this he worked into his own painting with his unique compositional technique. He had been well schooled in composition through fan painting and simply expanded this for larger surfaces.

The "Sekiya" and "Miotsukushi" screens in the Seikado are a lesson in the adaptation of painting from a fan surface to a screen. When this pair of screens is brought together, the place of juncture at the bottom becomes, as it were, the fan pivot, from which the figures are seen to radiate. The "Sekiya" screen shows Hikaru Genji, protagonist of the *Genji Monogatari*, as he visits the Ishiyama-dera temple and encounters his former lover Utsusemi. The "Miotsukushi" has Hikaru Genji once more, this time in a rendezvous with another former lover, Akashinoue.

Sotatsu arranged the various figures to accord with his sense of composition rather than to illustrate the progression of the story itself. The result is that he completely transformed the world of the classical *monogatari* by means of harmonious colors and artful arrangement. What holds the eye and moves the heart is not the interest of the story but its exquisite depiction. Sotatsu's was a completely new approach. Rather than call it a revival of classical Yamato-e, it would be more appropriate to call it the creation of an entirely new Yamato-e. It was Koetsu who focused attention on the classical past; but its re-creation was Sotatsu's achievement.

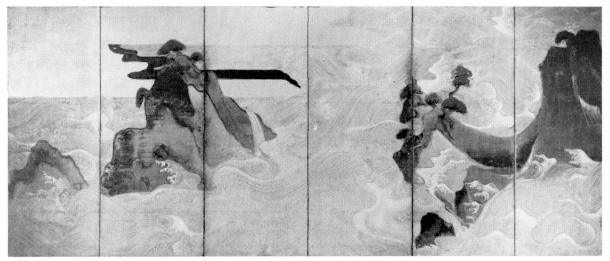

135. Tawaraya Sotatsu: Matsushima. *Pair of sixfold screens. Colors on gold foil over paper; dimensions of each screen: height, 166 cm.; width, 370 cm. Early seventeenth century. Freer Gallery of Art, Washington, D.C. (See also Figure 6.)*

The "Miotsukushi" painting bears the large seal of Sotatsu the *hokkyo,* which reads "Taiseiken." This means that the "Inen Sotatsu" of the Tawaraya had developed fully into the artist Sotatsu. And since he probably attained the rank of *hokkyo* in 1621, after executing his Yogen-in temple paintings, this work can be placed some time in the third decade of the seventeenth century.

THREE GREAT SCREENS   The two *Matsushima* screens (Figs. 6, 135) are among Sotatsu's masterpieces that are now abroad. They are in the Freer Gallery of Art in Washington, D.C. On the right as we face them are Sotatsu's signature and the Taiseiken seal. Besides this pair of screens there is supposed to have originally been another pair, the two pairs together illustrating the "Azuma Kudari" episode from the *Ise Monogatari.* The screens depict crags jutting out of wild waves in an abstract decorative treatment; again we notice the folding-fan composition. The special beauty of the work is the way the raging waves spill over the entire surface. Just as with his *Genji,* what interested Sotatsu here was not the *Ise Monogatari* so much as the composition of a scene.

For economy of composition and beauty of color, the *Bugaku* screens (Figs. 7, 67) in the Sambo-in at Daigo-ji temple are Sotatsu's finest. The right-hand screen depicts *Saisoro* (masked old man's dance) and *Nasori* (blue-masked dragon dance) dancers; the left-hand screen shows figures doing the *Genjogaku* (snake dance), *Raryo-o* (valiant king), and *Konron Hassen* (four cranes) dances. Sotatsu drew freely on such sources as Bugaku books and screens of the Muromachi period for his figures. As usual, he arranged them according to his fan-composition method. The figures radiate from the center, dancing across the gold ground toward the rear, just as if they were on a fan. At the top left the bases of pine and cherry trees and at the lower right the drums and curtain of the stage contribute to the impression of depth. This is a simple yet rigid composition. The dances unfold easily, but the dancers are not allowed to budge. The gold ground and brilliantly colored costumes seem to confront each other, yet always maintain a balanced equilibrium. This almost magical technique sums up all Sotatsu's painting secrets. *Bugaku* dates to about the time of Sotatsu's *Life of Priest Saigyo,* or 1630.

Next come the *God of Wind and God of Thunder*

136. *Tawaraya Sotatsu: cover (left) and frontis-piece (below) of* Heike Nokyo *hand scroll. Colors on paper; height, 26.3 cm.; width, 26 cm. 1602. Itsukushima Shrine, Hiroshima Prefecture.*

137. *Tawaraya Sotatsu: detail of the "Sekiya" scene from* Genji Monogatari. *Sixfold screen. Colors on gold foil over paper; dimensions of each screen: height, 81 cm.; width, 327 cm. Early seventeenth century.*

screens (Fig. 14). These deities, originally gods of India, are often seen in Buddhist art. Typical is the sculpture in the Sanjusangendo of Kyoto, with its fearsome gods flying through the skies. We meet them again in Yamato-e scrolls. In the *Kitano Tenjin Engi* scroll, for instance, the god of thunder is shown falling into the Seiryoden palace under the curse of Sugawara Michizane. Such were among Sotatsu's sources. In Figure 138 we see a fan of Sotatsu's on which is painted the god of thunder and a tower gate. In an *Ise Monogatari shikishi* (Fig. 139) this god is depicted as the demon of Akutagawa. Sotatsu's famous *God of Wind and God of Thunder* amalgamates all these models.

Again we see the influence of the fan-composition approach. The gods are depicted at the upper right and left, with the god of thunder's sash describing a fanlike arc. The middle portion is left empty; the center of gravity is at the bottom of this area, and the motion converges, reversing the usual radiation. The pivot of the fan seems to be reining in gods bent on flying off in opposite directions, endowing the whole with tremendous movement.

The broad, rich line shows Sotatsu's originality at work; the line remains but is almost surface-like in effect. The effect of the color arrangement of white, green, blue, red, and brown on the gold ground is one of quiet dignity; the billowing clouds, painted with *tarashikomi* blotching, are remarkably rendered.

Each time I find myself in front of it, I feel keenly how perfectly the word "masterpiece" fits this work. Is there any other painting as brilliant or as effervescent? It not only is Sotatsu's finest work but also ranks among the great works of world art. With it Sotatsu attained full maturity as both man and artist.

ANIMAL PAINTINGS   Large animals are a subject Sotatsu seems to have made a specialty. In the Yogen-in temple paintings there is not as much freedom as in the *God of Wind and God of Thunder* screens, but the same brightness and expansiveness are seen.

The temple was restored in 1621 by the wife of Hidetada, the second Tokugawa shogun. It is

138 (above). *Tawaraya Sotatsu:* God of Thunder. *Fan painting mounted on a panel of a pair of eightfold screens. Colors on paper; height, 19 cm.; width, 59 cm. Early seventeenth century. Imperial Household Collection. (See also Figure 2.)*

139 (right). *Tawaraya Sotatsu:* God of Thunder. *Shikishi from* Ise Monogatari. *Colors on paper; height, 24.7 cm.; width, 21 cm. Early seventeenth century.*

thought that Sotatsu was probably commissioned to do the door and wall paintings through the recommendation of Koetsu and Ogata Sohaku. The latter, who had established the Kariganeya, had close ties with the wife of Hidetada. He also maintained a residence in Takagamine.

Sotatsu executed this large-scale project, of which only the sliding doors with pines and the cedar doors with animals remain, in his typical style.

The animal paintings are particularly outstanding. White elephants (Fig. 38) occupy two panels and lions (Fig. 18) four. There are also rhinoceroses, by a student, on two panels. The elephant painting shown in Figure 38 fills the entire surface of the door, using the space masterfully. These doors are representative of Sotatsu's abstract decorative style, with its simple form and color and strong line.

SCROLLS AND BOOKS   In 1630 Sotatsu made two copies of the *Life of Priest Saigyo* scrolls (Figs. 15, 16, 42). The original used was the version of Kaida Unemenosuke Soho. Of the two copies by Sotatsu, one, formerly owned by the Mori family, has a colophon by Karasumaru Mitsuhiro (Fig. 141) that reads: "The foregoing painting is of the deeds of the Priest Saigyo. Four narrative scrolls, requested by Honda Tomimasa, Courtier of Izonokami. *Hokkyo* Sotatsu was duly commissioned to reproduce the original. I myself did the writing, a subject for derision. Early September in the seventh year of Kan'ei [1630]. Mitsuhiro. Senior grade, second class of court rank."

The Mori version (Fig. 15) is in four scrolls and has calligraphy by Mitsuhiro. In the Watanabe version (Fig. 16) there is no colophon, and the writing and painting are on three scrolls each. All the illustrations are copies, but with Sotatsu's free brushwork and colors they seem like altogether new paintings. The free, rich line and color provide a key to understanding the towering talent of Sotatsu.

There are extant forty-six folding scroll books of illustrations on *shikishi* paper. They include scenes from the *Ise Monogatari* (Figs. 19, 139), as well as text. There are several duplicate sets that have been broken up, which we may consider as typical of the fine work of the Tawaraya. None bears the calligraphy of Koetsu and some have no writing at all, which leads to the conclusion that the painting and writing were done at different times. The Tawaraya apparently did the painting on order, its clients adding writing when they wished.

140. *Tawaraya Sotatsu:* Mandarin Duck. *Hanging scroll. Ink on paper; height, 98.8 cm.; width, 42.4 cm. Early seventeenth century.*

INK PAINTING   Finally, we have Sotatsu's *sui-bokuga,* or ink paintings. There are countless such paintings attributed to him. However, very few reflect his high standards. The majority were produced in quantity in the Tawara-ya as *oshie-bari,* paintings to be affixed to screens. The subjects included flowers and grasses of the four seasons, great religious or supernatural figures, and animals.

Birds in a Lotus Pond (Fig. 47) is generally recognized as Sotatsu's masterpiece in this genre. A closer scrutiny of the india-ink technique and the deft, delicate touch shows us clearly the kind of feeling that must be attained for something to be a true Sotatsu piece. There is a warm bond with nature, a boundless affection for birds and flowers, and an amazing ability to express this feeling. Other artists have the technical ability. But the special appeal of Sotatsu is his affectionate handling, his really caring for his subject matter.

The ox painting of Figure 45 has these qualities. Again, there are artists who can as skillfully render rippling muscles and animal strength. But few look as affectionately as Sotatsu into the heart of the subject.

Tarashikomi and *tamekomi,* blotching techniques developed for color painting, are used to supreme effect in Sotatsu's color work and gold-and-silver underpainting. But he also carried them over into ink painting. His *suibokuga* are of course painted in black ink, but ink used with the same feeling as for color. As usual, Sotatsu's technique manifests something over and above technique: he is able to express an inner feeling that cannot be shown through line or surface painting alone. This indeed is the mark of the stature of his ink painting.

His *Ducks and Reeds* (Fig. 46) was once attached to a wall in the Muryoju-in at Daigo-ji temple but was later made into a pair of single-panel screens. The ducks, shown flying gracefully over withered reeds, have been captured with the beautiful, lifelike line of Sotatsu's brush. He did many other ink paintings of birds, but none as superb as this.

Daigo-ji also has the *Bugaku* screens and some of Sotatsu's screen-mounted fans. The *Genji* screens now in the Seikado were also formerly here. This has naturally led to conjecture that Sotatsu had close connections with the temple, but there is no recorded evidence of such. However, there is a single extant letter in Sotatsu's hand (Fig. 130), reading: "Thank you for your most wonderful gift. I am grateful for your letter and the five bamboo

141. *Karasumaru Mitsuhiro: colophon of* Life of Priest Saigyo *hand scroll with paintings by Sotatsu. Height, 33.4 cm. 1630. Formerly in the Mori Collection.*

shoots from Daigo-ji that you sent me. Your kindness leaves me beholden beyond words. I came and left so soon that there was no time to talk, leaving us with much unsaid. I hope that at the next opportunity you will drop in for a talk. When you do, I shall express my gratitude more adequately."

The letter is addressed to Kaian. This Kaian may have been Takaya Soetsu, the personal physician of Date Masamune, a warrior-diplomat and patron of the arts. Or he may have been the famed Kyoto doctor Yoshida Kaian, whom Sotatsu writes to thank for a present of bamboo shoots from Daigo-ji. Sotatsu's having had ties with the temple does not necessarily follow, but the letter is interesting and invites speculation. Yoshida Kaian belonged to the Kyoto upper-class *machishu*. Since he was acquainted with Karasumaru Mitsuhiro, he was also connected with Sotatsu and his world. Thus, this letter serves as added information on Sotatsu and the society in which he circulated.

CHAPTER ELEVEN

The Works of Korin

INK PAINTING   Korin's ink paintings are a good vantage point from which to view his art. Ink mirrors the artist. This is especially true of Sotatsu and Korin. As artists, their most representative works are decorative paintings on large surfaces with a gold ground. Their ink painting, on the other hand, would seem to show more clearly their personalities and human qualities.

This is because an ink painting is executed with a single, irreversible pass of the brush that reveals the artist's character. What a painting might hide behind color and decorative art conceal behind stylized forms is utterly revealed in ink. This is even more marked with Korin than Sotatsu.

Korin's ink painting, including that on Kenzan's pottery, shows that, unlike Sotatsu, he did not handle color and ink with the same feeling. Korin did not make much use of contourless methods, either. In fact, he thought highly of line painting, the fundamentals of which he apparently owed to the Kano school. His studies as a young man, under the Kano-school master Yamamoto Soken, were brief, but he learned to appreciate the uses of line and black ink for direct, personal expression. These techniques he developed into his soft, Sotatsu-like line.

Korin's line is facile and swift, the manifestation of his talent and skill. Facile but not careless, swift but not slipshod, it has a grace compounded of refined taste and vitality, qualities basic to both his ink painting and his character. They are seen best

in his *Bamboo and Plum* screens (Fig. 50) and in the square dish with a painting of bamboo (Fig. 72). The bold, fresh composition of the screens is seen in the placement of light and dark bamboo against the gold ground. The swift, crisp line of leaves and branches is worlds away from the reserved rendering of Sotatsu. Korin epitomizes the elegance and dash of Genroku. The naturalistic rendition of the bamboo and plum through ink-painting techniques demonstrates the superb feeling that Korin brings to his decorative screens.

As I have already pointed out, in contrast to the works just discussed, there are others that contain a strange shadow. This group, typified by the *Vimalakirti* painting (Fig. 89), displays Korin's not very veiled contempt for the world in which he lived. *Pu Tai Playing Kickball* (Fig. 51) falls into the same category. This appears to be his earliest extant work, judging by the seal. We can probably date it to about 1697, before he attained the rank of *hokkyo* in 1701, whereas *Vimalakirti* is thought to have been painted much later. Thus we are compelled to see this shadow as the constant companion of Korin's career, now and then showing through his work.

Korin's dark side shows most in his figure painting, while the brighter Korin is seen in his nature themes or where man associates with nature. Examples are the *Bamboo and Plum* screens, *Tiger in the Bamboo* (Fig. 146), *Li Po at the Waterfall*, and the dish with Huang Shan-ku watching sea gulls (Fig. 86). But where people alone appear, just as surely enters

142. *Ogata Korin: Azaleas. Hanging scroll. Ink and light colors on silk; height, 39.6 cm.; width, 60.5 cm. Early eighteenth century.*

some shadow. Examples of this are *T'ai Kung-wang Fishing* (Fig. 93), *Ch'in Kao Riding a Carp,* the hexagonal dish with a painting of Shou Lao (Fig. 79), and the square dish depicting Shih-te (Fig. 3).

If "shadow" misses the mark in describing Korin's somber side, we might call it a certain perverse or twisted feeling. *Pu Tai* and *Ch'in Kao* surely have this twist. And it is even plainer in *Vimalakirti.* As I have mentioned earlier, we have here sometimes Korin's reflection of a soft, overripe culture, sometimes his strong reaction against it, and sometimes an expression of disgust. Korin's antipathy on occasion poisons his palette to the point of making even his gods and sages join in the protest. This tendency becomes ever stronger with the passage of time.

Korin leaves us one portrait painted with all his heart, that of Nakamura Kuranosuke (Fig. 92). Kuranosuke had always been close to Korin, appreciated his work, and even gave his daughter Okatsu in marriage to Korin's son Jujiro. An official of the Kyoto mint, he was known to the Genroku elite as Fujiwara Nobumitsu. Implicated in a financial scandal together with Fukae Shozaemon, Kuranosuke was banished in 1714 to Miyakejima, a small island off Japan. He was later pardoned and returned to Kyoto, where he died in 1730 at over sixty years of age. The legend on Korin's portrait of Kuranosuke indicates that it was painted early in 1704. The proper, refined rendering, a near-perfect example of Yamato-e portraiture, gives us a true-to-life picture of a fellow Genroku dandy.

FLORAL THEMES Korin's development of his specialty, the floral genre, began with his work in textile designs at the Kariganeya (Fig. 148). Among a number of study sketches from the shop in notebook form, now in the possession of the Konishi family (into which his son Juichiro was adopted), we find many patterns with flowers, designed in the rich Genroku style. They include Korin's special loves: plum, autumn grass, and iris designs. It would be only natural for Korin, surrounded by clothing of such beautiful floral patterns, to feel attracted to *soka,* the genre of flowers and grasses.

143 (left). *Ogata Korin: round fan with painting of autumn grasses. Colors on paper; height, 23.3 cm.; width, 24.2 cm. Early eighteenth century.*

144 (right). *Ogata Korin: round fan with painting of bracken. Colors on paper; height, 24.6 cm.; width, 24.4 cm. Ear v eighteenth century.*

It has been mentioned that Korin's work in this field had a marked tendency toward Sosetsu's kind of decorativeness. He departs decisively from Sosetsu, however, in the firm realism underlying his decorative patterning. His sketches (Figs. 96, 97) and scrolls (Figs. 76, 90) show this realism and also how Korin modeled his painting after Sotatsu's flowers-and-grasses work. What he shared of Sotatsu's naturalism served to keep him free of the prosaic formalism of Sosetsu-style decorative painting. To corroborate this, we have only to look at his *Azaleas* (Fig. 142) or his round-fan paintings of floral themes (Figs. 143, 144).

Azaleas is painted in india ink and light colors. The red of the azaleas in particular is a rare and haunting color. Korin's love for the flowers blooming in the shadow of a rock, and his decorative blending of brook and banks, result in a delightful compositional give-and-take. In addition to talent, a sensitivity to decorative and naturalistic elements alike is necessary in order to harmonize them so gracefully. Korin had both talent and sensitivity in ample measure and never had to strain to call them

forth; his brush seemed to move almost spontaneously in the right direction. This is seen clearly in several recently discovered flower-and-bird paintings on incense wrappers and in his *Thousand Cranes* (Fig. 69), which seems to have been based on a gold-and-silver underpainting of plovers by Sotatsu. Korin's birds are much more beautiful, decoratively speaking, than Sotatsu's; they mark him as an artist of singularly rich gifts and deep feeling.

Korin's round fans are indicative of how alive nature can be within the framework of decorative design. His paintings of bracken (Fig. 144), hollyhocks, bamboo (Fig. 94), white plum, autumn grasses (Fig. 143), the maples of Tatsutagawa (Fig. 75), and the *yatsuhashi* show his great virtuosity in composing for this shape, rivaling Sotatsu's use of folding-fan composition. Korin came to know and love circular treatment, and thus the round-fan shape, through his work with circular textile designs; one can imagine the relish with which he painted them, each so different from the others. This circular composition greatly influenced his brother Kenzan's pottery painting, as well.

145 (below). *Ogata Korin: "Yatsuhashi" scene from* Ise Monogatari. *Hanging scroll. Colors on paper; height, 95.7 cm.; width, 43.3 cm. Early eighteenth century. Tokyo National Museum.*

TWO GREAT SCREENS It is not known just when Korin painted the *Irises* (Fig. 73) and *Red and White Plum Blossoms* (Figs. 70, 71) screens, but their accomplished quality makes it evident that they followed most of his paintings of similar subjects. The *Irises* screens reduce his *yatsuhashi* theme to its simplest component, the irises.

Iris motifs appear often in Korin's textile designs, round fans, hanging scrolls, and screens. First, in his version of the "Yatsuhashi" scene from the *Ise Monogatari* (Fig. 145), we see Narihira and his attendants at a river, pausing before crossing to gaze at the banks festooned with irises. Then the figures fade and the bridge disappears, leaving us at last with only the clusters of flowers of the *Irises* screens. The composition and colors, reduced to barest simplicity, push Korin's idea of decoration to its limit. What keeps him from falling into Sosetsu's mannerism, however, is the astonishing realism of his treatment. His flowers have none of the clinging sentimentality of the *Ise Monogatari*. It is simply the irises themselves that are stressed. They look almost like cutouts arranged on the surface of the screen. The treatment is low-keyed and precise, and because of this the flowers remain real.

Red and White Plum Blossoms is Korin's best pair o

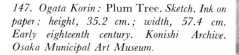

146. *Ogata Korin:* Tiger in the Bamboo. *Hanging scroll. Ink on paper; height, 28.3 cm.; width, 39 cm. Early eighteenth century.*

147. *Ogata Korin:* Plum Tree. Sketch. *Ink on paper; height, 35.2 cm.; width, 57.4 cm. Early eighteenth century. Konishi Archive. Osaka Municipal Art Museum.*

screens, and one of the best in Japanese decorative art, along with Sotatsu's *God of Wind and God of Thunder.* Flowing beneath the blossoming red and white plum trees is a thawing, swirling stream—an old standby in Yamato-e. Korin sought to capture its lyricism in the realm of decorative art. *Red and White Plum Blossoms* blends strict realism with stylized beauty. The flow of the stream is completely unified by swirling decorative patterns, the so-called "Korin waves," the most beautiful and forceful of all Japanese water depictions. Here Korin surpassed himself. The painting of the stream was effected by applying alum mixed with glue on raised silver foil, oxidizing it with sulphur, then painting it silver. This shows how far Korin would go to obtain just the right effect.

The water theme in Korin's *Waves* (Fig. 74) results in another great screen painting. Dark waters rage; white billows, like bared teeth, rise out of the sea. This is a stark, powerful depiction with excellent brushwork in the ink-painting style. The work lacks the abstraction we see in *Red and White Plum Blossoms* with its "Korin waves." The roll of the sea is stopped for a marvelous moment, and the roar of the waves is almost audible. We have seen figure painting in ink that shows Korin's peculiar twist, telling us of his dislikes. *Waves* and *Red and White*

Plum Blossoms, through their strength and straightforward treatment, are in some way a transference or sublimation of the deeply personal protest that is so much a part of Korin.

LACQUERWARE AND KIMONO

Korin was a man of many talents. Borrowing the first character of Koetsu's name for his own name, he was Koetsu's successor in gold-lacquer work. The "Yatsuhashi" and "Suminoe" lacquer boxes (Fig. 91) do not have the strength of Koetsu's work but are charming creations, all the same. The writing box with the fan-painting applique seen in Figures 78 and 99 is much more Korin-like; several round and folding fans are adroitly arranged both inside and outside the box. The beauty of the painting and the artful arrangement make for a superb decorative effect. Because not all the paintings are by Korin, some believe that the fans were affixed to the box later by someone else. However, the whole idea is so like Korin that I think it likely to be his creation.

Finally, to show how Korin set the style in Genroku fashion, let us look at his Fuyuki *kosode* (short-sleeved kimono; Fig. 77). He probably made it for the Fuyuki family in 1704 while in Edo. He seems to have done a considerable amount of original

148. Circular designs from the Kariganeya album. Ink on paper. Late seventeenth century.

garment painting. The Genroku genre novel *Ko-shoku Fumi Denju* (A Chronicle of Love) mentions Korin's ink painting of a pine on a white crepe satin kimono, indicating that Korin originals had caught on in fashionable circles. These added an item to the Kariganeya sales line around the time that *Yuzen-zome* textiles were popular.

By turning out luxurious hand-painted kimono and making them a vogue in upper-class circles, I think, Korin was trying to reinforce *machishu* feelings of superiority over the rising class of bourgeois merchants. By now most families of the old elite had been debilitated through loans to daimyo, as had the Kariganeya. A new class of calculating, grasping merchants had emerged, and gaudily patterned *Yuzen-zome* garments evinced its tastes. This situation undoubtedly fueled Korin's anger. I take his garment painting to be a byproduct of this.

CHAPTER TWELVE

The Works of Kenzan

THE NARUTAKI PERIOD   Kenzan's creative period lasted for over forty years, beginning with the Narutaki kiln in 1699 and ending only with his death in 1743. Because he produced pottery, his output considerably exceeded that of a painter. Nevertheless, his work should not for that reason be judged by milder standards than if he had been a painter. Kenzan was only human, and from time to time, like other artists, he produced poor-quality work. This may be so, but we should not indulge in false sympathy for him. An artist should be judged on the heights he attains, not on the depths to which his work may occasionally sink. In considering the work of one who has committed his life to art, we should ignore anything that is not beautiful; and this should hold especially for Kenzan.

In sifting through his work in this light, most of the pieces attributed to Kenzan that date from his difficult times, which have hitherto been seen as typical, should be rejudged according to different criteria. This is true, for example, of his "Yatsuhashi" and "Floral Bouquet" pieces, with their unnaturalness and poor quality; they are dubious inclusions as typical Kenzan works.

KENZAN'S POTTERY-MAKING at Narutaki started with Korin doing the painting. These works can be divided into two categories: pieces from about 1700–1701, and those of a decade later, around 1711. This breakdown is made on the basis of Korin's style and signature. Representative of the latter category is the hexagonal dish with a painting of Shou Lao, the god of longevity (Fig. 79). The products of the earlier period are exemplified by the square dish with waves and plovers (Fig. 87).

The later period also includes the dish with the poet Huang Shan-ku watching sea gulls (Figs. 86, 107) and a set of ten square dishes with paintings of figures, floral themes, and birds, to which the dish with the bamboo painting (Fig. 72) belongs. All the above feature Korin's painting with Kenzan's calligraphy and edge trim. But we cannot see in them Kenzan's own quality as artist-craftsman, whereby he developed his new and distinctive pottery style.

In 1701 Korin became a *hokkyo* and soon after went to Edo, leaving Kenzan to run the Narutaki kiln alone. The man later to be acclaimed as Japan's greatest potter now had on hand the sketches Korin had left him to work with; he began doing his own painting, and with time and much effort gradually came into his own.

Some Narutaki pieces have painting by Watanabe Shiko, Korin's disciple, and writing by Kenzan. But among those we must attribute exclusively to Kenzan are his "Waterfall" (Figs. 80, 150) and "Plum Blossoms" (Fig. 149) tea bowls with verses on them. His ink-painting technique has a much stronger Chinese style than does Korin's, and does not show Kenzan's later fusion of this style with Yamato-e. But we do sense Kenzan's inner vitality, the soul of a man of culture who could shut out the

149. *Ogata Kenzan: two views of "Plum Blossoms" tea bowl. Rust painting; diameter, 10.2 cm. Early eighteenth century.*

world for a while. The script also has a slightly stiff Chinese style. Not yet bursting forth freely into the decorative, it conscientiously adheres to form.

The "rust-painting" technique, together with the color-painting methods learned from Ninsei, resulted in Kenzan's fresh, graceful, original pottery. With his famous plum-blossom incense container and his painted earthenware dishes, he seems to have begun experimenting with many techniques and shapes—tea bowls, water containers, incense bowls, sakè cups, and plates. He did not stick to Yamato-e style, either, but experimented with Delft, Kochi-yaki (Cochin China ware), Sungkalok (a ware now made in Chiengmai, Thailand), and Arita ware. He appears to have made a project of ceramic study.

His crosshatched incense container with plum blossoms (Fig. 108) is considered the best of these wares. Although it is made with a mold, the shape of the container and treatment of the handle show rich feeling. Kenzan's weak point as a craftsman, the molding, is fairly well overcome here. The plums, in rust and white, seem to bathe the whole piece in their bloom and perfume. It is an exquisite work, small but of exceptional quality.

His lily-shaped bowl (Fig. 109), with its simplicity, typifies Kenzan's earliest ceramic work. The interesting, appealing shape is peculiar to him. The unassuming line of the petals also conveys something of his personality.

The kingfisher and lotus in relief on a black Raku ware tea bowl (Fig. 104) and his "Waterfall" tea bowl with its bold ink painting are both generally placed in the Narutaki period because of their youthful, robust feeling and still-imperfect technique. (His black Raku methods are not recorded in his recipes in deference to the Raku family.) Kenzan surely made a few pieces of this kind for his own pleasure, probably with Koetsu in mind. The painting and writing on the "Waterfall" tea bowl, as on the "Plum Blossoms" tea bowl, show Kenzan on the threshold of an important stage in his ceramic achievements.

The Narutaki period was the earliest stage of Kenzan's art. At times his vision exceeded his technique, and the resultant failures were not few. Nevertheless, we should judge the many Narutaki Kenzan products according to strict standards, singling out the very best, as I mentioned before; we must try to understand what Kenzan was aiming

150. *Ogata Kenzan: "Waterfall" tea bowl. Rust painting; diameter, 10.3 cm. Early eighteenth century. (See also Figure 80.)*

151. *Ogata Kenzan: signature on foot of bowl with painting of red and white plum blossoms. Diameter, 20.2 cm. 1737. (See also Figure 83.)*

for and then evaluate each piece on the basis of whether it achieves these ends. With this in mind I would not call this Kenzan's greatest period.

The fact is that Kenzan's artistic temperament was probably what made the Narutaki kiln operation a commercial failure. The dish with the poet Huang Shan-ku, made in about 1711, has a high-flown inscription on the back (Fig. 107) that reads: "Made in the atelier of Deep Reflection, Kenzan the potter, in southern Kyoto, in the Great Nation of Japan." Over the years the Narutaki kiln operation, begun as a business, became more and more an artistic laboratory. It is easy to suppose that, far from providing him with a living, the kiln ran him well into the red.

In the legends on the reverse of the Huang Shan-ku and god of wealth dishes are inscriptions of the characters for "Kenzan" and "Shinsho" like those on the *Pine on Tea Bowl* painting (Fig. 81). He probably executed this work as a kind of under-painting, yet it is a lyrical and lovely piece. There were probably bowls exactly like it in the pottery made in his later Narutaki period. From the gold painting on the pine branches one wonders if he may have attempted gold-painted pottery, too.

But more important, the date on the seal of the painting tells us that it is from his later Narutaki period. It is a small piece, yet the treatment here supplies us with almost the only Kyoto Kenzan painting worthy of the name.

THE CHOJIYAMACHI PERIOD

Very little of Kenzan's work at Chojiyamachi strikes us as truly fine art; hence this book includes no color reproductions of pieces from this period. Kenzan was unhappy turning out dinnerware for the general public, although it resulted in a vogue for Kenzan ware. He took orders for designs he did not want to do but had to, for the markets near his kiln in Awataguchi and Gojosaka. It became impossible for him to throw himself wholeheartedly into his work. Korin's death in 1716 probably also sapped some of his artistic initiative.

Just barely within his standards is the "Diadem" oblong dish (Fig. 103) and a group of round dishes with green ground and white plum blossoms formed by leaving the ground unpainted. There is a considerable amount of Chojiyamachi work of about this standard.

152. Ogata Kenzan: two views of "Musashino" water jar. Colors; height, 17.5 cm. 1737.

THE EDO YEARS   Kenzan's move to Edo in 1731 marked a turning point in his career. Thanks to Prince Kokan's patronage, he was soon able to build a kiln at Iriya, and in the meantime he probably devoted himself to painting. It was after Iriya and especially after the sojourn in Sano that he took up painting in earnest. A number of pieces inscribed with the date and various names for Kyoto—Keicho, Karaku, Heianjo—are extant. Those regarded as having authentic signatures are not so many; but even so, they indicate the legacy of Kenzan's painting efforts in Edo.

The great fire of Edo in 1737, while Kenzan was in Sano, destroyed much of the work he had done there, and frequent fires in the time that followed were to wipe out nearly all of it, both pottery and painting. The almost total blank this leaves us for the period is one reason for the sudden difference

we note when we come across his Sano work. Nevertheless, we can point to several fine pieces from Kenzan's Edo period.

One is the hanging scroll seen in Figure 48. This is a simple depiction of camellias, signed with Kenzan's later art name, Shisui Rokan Shinsho (Fig. 154). This piece indicates how Kenzan had adapted his Chinese-painting style; the piece is replete with the kind of Yamato-e feeling we find in Sotatsu's ink painting. The ink tones and the supple line of the leaves clearly show him to have completely rid himself of the rigidity of the Narutaki period and to be developing his own distinctive painting style. The signature also shows his own style; the calligraphy of Kenzan's later life has taken form.

The other work is his *Snake Gourd* painting (Fig. 49), thought to be a little later than the camellia

153 (left). Ogata Kenzan: inscription on back of square dish with painting of god of wealth. Rust painting; height, 21.8 cm.; width, 21.7 cm. Early eighteenth century. Fujita Art Museum, Osaka.

154 (right). Ogata Kenzan: signature and seal on Camellias hanging scroll. Ink on paper. C. mid-eighteenth century. (See also Figure 48).

painting. The brushwork is a magnificent blend of the richness of Sotatsu and the crispness of Korin. *Snake Gourd* was probably painted in the mid-1730's, after the Iriya kiln was built. The art Kenzan had cultivated at Narutaki and had held in reserve in Chojiyamachi was now finally about to bloom, as these two paintings indicate. Few works of art show this happy blend of seasoned hand and youthful heart. Through them we see clearly the inevitable development of Kenzan's Sano style.

SANO KENZAN We have long had Kenzan's *Sano Densho* (Sano Recipes) and a number of Sano Kenzan pieces. Formerly it was difficult to establish whether all such pottery was actually by Kenzan's hand. His stay in Sano itself was recognized, but the nature and duration of his work there were unknown. But recently a great number of pieces have been found, and Kenzan's Sano diaries (Figs. 106, 111, 113) have been discovered, leaving more details open to view.

During more than a year's sojourn in Sano, Kenzan probably employed nearly all the techniques he had used during his Iriya kiln days. Here we have painting and script, in both the Chinese and Japanese styles, developed into his fullest achievements as artist-ceramist. This work is decorative painting carefully grounded in realism; yet, its decorative character notwithstanding, it also has the elegant élan of the *bunjinga* (literati painting) genre.

All the color plates of his masterpieces from this period display Kenzan's strong points. The square dish with camellias in Figure 82, called a *nishinbachi*, has a shape often seen in Aizu-Hongo kiln products. It is a lovely piece, with white, yellow, and red camellias on a green ground done in the wax-resist technique. Kenzan often tried the wax-resist method, and this piece is its most effective realization. The green is complex and full of interesting variation, and the "modern" look of the modeling is attractive.

The lotus dish (Fig. 84) is a masterpiece of Kenzan's ink painting on pottery. It is based on Sotatsu's *Birds in a Lotus Pond* (Fig. 47); other works copy this painting exactly. The inscription *Jakumetsu joshin*, on the upper right of the dish, is a superb example of Kenzan's calligraphy, with its unity of decorative quality and feeling and its harmony with the composition of the painting. From Kenzan's diaries it is clear that of his aristocratic hosts at Sano, it was Sudo Tosen whom Kenzan held in greatest affection. The gifts Kenzan presented to him were of superb workmanship, as the lotus dish demonstrates.

The "Thistle" tea bowl (Fig. 105) also has a timeless appeal. Kenzan made many tea bowls, and their paintings show many and varied techniques. This bowl has only a single plant in indigo; but one look at it tells us how much Kenzan loved wild flowers. This piece crystallizes his poetic sensibility.

The bowl with red and white plum blossoms (Figs. 83, 151) is another masterpiece, combining Kenzan's poetic feeling and the sensuous beauty of Genroku. The riot of red and white blossoms on this bowl is the most beautiful of all his plum paintings and has a vitality not found in any of Korin's depictions. The blossoms are so real that Kenzan himself seems to be reaching out to us from among them. The characters reading *ga shin*, written in the center of the bowl, express the feeling of the piece: "elegant intimacy."

This kind of work, bringing together painting, calligraphy, and pottery, makes up the world of Kenzan, a personal world quite inimitable by any other artist. He immersed himself in it, attuned to nature and lost in a love for flowers. His script, his painting, his pottery reflect the poetry in his heart. Pure poetry like his speaks to us. Technique and dazzling skill hold our attention for a time. But the pure heart of Kenzan claims our hearts forever.

TITLES IN THE SERIES

Although the individual books in the series are designed as self-contained units, so that readers may choose subjects according to their personal interests, the series itself constitutes a full survey of Japanese art and is therefore a reference work of great value. The titles are listed below in the same order, roughly chronological, as those of the original Japanese versions, with the addition of the index volume.

The "weathermark" identifies this book as having been planned, designed, and produced at the Tokyo offices of John Weatherhill, Inc., 7-6-13 Roppongi, Minato-ku, Tokyo 106. Book design and typography by Meredith Weatherby and Ronald V. Bell. Layout of photographs by Suzanne Trumbull. Composition by General Printing Co., Yokohama. Color plates engraved and printed by Nissha Printing Co., Kyoto, and Hanshich Printing Co., Tokyo. Gravure plates engraved and printed by Inshokan Printing Co., Tokyo. Monochrome letterpress platemaking and printing and text printing by Toyo Printing Co., Tokyo. Bound at the Makoto Binderies, Tokyo. Text is set in 10-pt. Monotype Baskerville with hand-set Optima for display.